# REPAY
## AS YOU EARN

# REPAY AS YOU EARN

The Flawed Government Program
to Help Students Have
Public Service Careers

PHILIP G. SCHRAG

**BERGIN & GARVEY**
Westport, Connecticut • London

**Library of Congress Cataloging-in-Publication Data**

Schrag, Philip G., 1943–
    Repay as you earn : the flawed government program to help students have public
service careers / Philip G. Schrag.
      p.  cm.
    Includes bibliographical references (p.  ) and index.
    ISBN 0–89789–834–6 (alk. paper)
    1. Student loan funds—United States.  2. Federal aid to higher education—United
States.  3. Educational law and legislation—United States.  I. Title.
LB2340.2.S38  2002
378.3'62'0973—dc21     2001035641

British Library Cataloguing in Publication Data is available.

Library of Congress Catalog Card Number: 2001035641
ISBN: 0–89789–834–6

First published in 2002

Bergin & Garvey, 88 Post Road West, Westport, CT 06881
An imprint of Greenwood Publishing Group, Inc.
www.greenwood.com

Printed in the United States of America

The paper used in this book complies with the
Permanent Paper Standard issued by the National
Information Standards Organization (Z39.48–1984).

10 9 8 7 6 5 4 3 2 1

**Copyright Acknowledgments**

The author and publisher are grateful to the following for granting permission to reprint
from their materials:

Philip G. Schrag, *The Federal Income-Contingent Repayment Option for Law Student Loans*, 29
HOFSTRA L. REV. 733 (2001).

**For John R. Kramer**

with appreciation for his efforts, over many decades,
to make education more affordable for students committed to
public service

# Contents

# Acknowledgments

I am very deeply indebted first and foremost to Ruth Lammert-Reeves, Georgetown's outstanding assistant dean for financial aid, for helping to educate me about loan repayment plans and options and for guiding me to many helpful documentary materials. In the course of talking with other law school financial aid advisors, I learned how much Ms. Lammert-Reeves is admired in her professional community, and I came to understand the well-deserved basis of her high standing there.

The research for this book was supported in part by a grant from the Open Society Institute, and in part by writing grants from Georgetown University Law Center, which were made available by Dean Judith C. Areen. I am grateful for both sources of assistance.

I also appreciate the enormously important contributions of my student research assistants, Lewis Walton, Benjamin Gardner, and Tai-yeu Hsia. Thanks are due as well to Professor Lisa Lerman of Catholic University Law School, who distributed my student questionnaire at her institution; the hundreds of students at Georgetown and Catholic Universities who responded to the questionnaire; the ninety-eight financial aid advisors and fifty-seven directors of legal aid offices and public interest law firms who answered the questionnaires I sent them; and several officials of the Department of Education who took time to explain to Mr. Hsia and me the methods of the Department's income-contingent calculations. I also appreciate the outstanding work of Decision Research, Inc., which computed the data from the student and financial aid advisor surveys, and the expert assistance of John Showalter and Anna Selden, who helped to prepare this book for publication. Finally, I am grateful for the valuable comments made by Stephen Brown, David Jaffe, Elliott Milstein, Daniel L. Pollard, Mark Kantrowitz, and members of Georgetown's faculty scholarship workshop on earlier drafts of the manuscript.

## THE FINAID.ORG WEBSITE

I am very happy to have collaborated with Mark Kantrowitz, founder of FinAid.org. FinAid is a nonprofit, public interest distributor of loan information for students; it provides a clear, up-to-date explanation of student loans and various calculators through which students can compute monthly payments and total costs of various types of loans. Mr. Kantrowitz created, and posted on FinAid.org, a Web-based version of the income-contingent loan calculator that Mr. Hsia and I developed so that the charts in chapter 5 could be compiled. The FinAid income-contingent repayment calculator is located at www.finaid.org/calculators/icr.phtml. If for some reason that website ceases to be operational, the Hsia-Schrag Microsoft Excel spreadsheet, through which the same calculations can be performed, is posted at http://data.law.georgetown.edu/faculty/schrag/loanrepayment.html. The FinAid version is, however, much more user friendly and is therefore recommended by the author.

This research was originally published in the spring 2001 issue of the *Hofstra Law Review*.[1]

## NOTE

1. Philip G. Schrag, *The Federal Income-Contingent Repayment Option for Law Student Loans*, 29 HOFSTRA L. REV. 733 (2001).

# Introduction

Many students complete graduate and professional school with very high educational debt. For some, the debt can without exaggeration be described as "staggering," in the sense that repayment according to a "standard" ten-year schedule would leave the graduate with full-time employment but scant discretionary income, able to survive only by sacrificing consumer goods and services, postponing having a home and a family, and accruing additional credit card debt. The loan repayment problem is greatest for those who would like to be self-sacrificing up to a reasonable point: those who decide to obtain graduate or professional educations because they want to serve the public, even if this means that they will have to accept much lower salaries than they might earn in private employment. Only as they accumulate the significant debt that often accompanies graduate education do they realize that loan repayment obligations significantly increase the pressure to take high-paying private sector jobs. As graduation approaches, many of these students feel, with some bitterness, that because of their debt, they have no choice but to abandon their original goals and seek employment with large corporate organizations.

In 1993, with strong encouragement from the new president, Bill Clinton, Congress seemed to come to the aid of graduates who faced the prospect of high debt and low incomes. When it established a program of direct lending to students by the U.S. Department of Education, it created an "income-contingent repayment option" through which annual repayment of most educational debt would be capped at a fraction of the graduate's income. The option would be available to all graduates. Students who paid through this plan for many years might temporarily accumulate mounting indebtedness because of the income-based cap on repayment. But the remaining debt would be canceled after twenty-five years of capped repayments. Furthermore, the graduates of schools that did not participate in the government's direct lending program could take advantage of the option through a consolidation loan from the federal government after graduation.

Shortly after its enactment, this new law was hailed as a "radical" change.[1] According to the Steven Waldman, the *Newsweek* legislative correspondent who closely followed the progress of this legislation so that he could write a book about its progress through Congress, the law "meant [that] anyone who still hadn't paid off their loan by year twenty-five would get an enormous gift from the taxpayers. The biggest benefit of all would go to . . . doctors who work in low-income clinics or lawyers who become public defenders—in other words, those doing the public service jobs Clinton admired."[2]

Eight years later, despite these apparent attractions, the income-contingent repayment option seems not to have caught on among those who attend high-cost graduate and professional schools. Is neglect of this program[3] justified by its economic disadvantages or the availability of good substitutes? Or is it based at least in part on noneconomic factors such as lack of information about its availability, the difficulty of computing the total cost of income-contingent borrowing, distrust of the federal government, or fear of unconventional financial devices? To put it another way, in the future, should students who are graduating with very high debt loads consider signing up for income-contingent repayment if they would prefer to have public service careers? If the income-contingent repayment option is not living up to its promises, at least for significant numbers of high-debt, low-income public servants, how should it be changed?

This book examines the promise, and to a large extent the failure, of the income-contingent repayment plan as it applies to the graduates who have the highest ratio of debt to income. The group on which I focus consists of those who want to become public interest lawyers. These men and women attend the nation's high-priced law schools because they want to take jobs as legal aid lawyers for indigent clients, public defenders, and local government officials. They are willing to accept jobs paying $25,000 to $32,000 per year when they could be earning more than $150,000 in large corporate firms. Even though these students are willing to give up the financial opportunities of private sector careers, they are stopped in their tracks by the educational debt, often more than $100,000, that they have accumulated. Under ordinary repayment plans, they cannot take public service jobs unless they are willing to starve in garrets.

Chapter 1 explores the amount of indebtedness and the expected incomes of recent law graduates. It examines the historic and recent literature on the extent of their debt, relating the current economic situation of indebted law graduates to the trends of tuition and debt in recent decades. Chapter 2 reviews the objectives and history of the legislation establishing an income-contingent loan repayment option. The legislative history demonstrates a broad consensus in favor of assisting students who planned public interest careers. Chapter 2 also explains the mechanics of income-contingent repayment and debt forgiveness under the law and its implementing regulations.

Chapters 3 and 4 provide empirical information about the response to the new federal program. Chapter 3 reports the results of my survey of law students' knowledge of the income-contingent repayment option and, to the extent that they know about it, their attitudes about this method of payment. Because students in most schools must rely on law school financial aid advisors for information and counseling about loan repayment options, chapter 4 reports the results of my survey of law school financial aid advisors' awareness of and beliefs about income-contingent repayment. These surveys provide statistical evidence supporting the hypothesis that this program is poorly understood and little used by one of the important constituencies for whom it was intended.

The surveys reveal that whereas neither students nor financial aid advisors are well informed about the income-contingent repayment option, those within each group who are informed shun it, though for different reasons. Students dislike it primarily because it requires at least an initial commitment to a twenty-five-year repayment schedule. Financial aid advisors are skeptical of it because they believe that few graduates would use it long enough to obtain its promised subsidies. However, 52 percent of the financial aid advisors believe that income-contingent repayment could be useful for at least 5 percent of their schools' recent graduates.

Having surveyed in chapters 3 and 4 the background of opinions about this program and the sources of the respondents' misgivings, I look in chapter 5 at the income-contingent repayment option from the perspective of some hypothetical recent graduates unhampered by either a lack of information about the program or distortions of its cost. From the perspective of hypothetical law students with high debt and different plans for long-term and short-term public service, I demonstrate the advantages and disadvantages of income-contingent repayment compared with standard repayment and with other long-term repayment plans. I also consider the effect of the availability of a law school loan repayment assistance plan, and of marriage, on the value of using income-contingent repayment. In addition, I direct students to a new website through which they may make their own personal calculations of how they would fare under the income-contingent plan, and through which they can compare income-contingent and standard repayments. Chapter 5 may enable future law students to make more rational debt repayment and career decisions, and it may help financial aid advisors to offer more sophisticated guidance.

In chapter 6, I ask why a plan that has been part of the federal law for more than five years, and that could help make loan repayment affordable for law graduates most in need of assistance, is so little understood or used. The existence of alternative payment reduction plans does not adequately explain the orphan status of income-contingent repayment. I consider, as well, inadequacies in the program itself; the impact of private lender hostility to the program and of partisan politics; and the poor quality of public information issued by the U.S. Department of Education.

In chapter 7, I make recommendations to students, to financial aid advisors, and to policy makers in Congress, the White House, and the Department of Education. I offer students some advice on financial planning within the constraints of the existing loan repayment system, and I encourage financial aid advisors to become more familiar with how income-contingent repayment can be useful for graduates with the highest debt and lowest incomes, particularly those who are committed to a lifetime of full-time public service. On the assumption that policy makers are now or will in the future be guided by the same desire to encourage public service that motivated legislators and President Clinton to create income-contingent repayment in 1993, I make several suggestions for making this program more attractive and more visible to borrowers who desire to become public interest lawyers.

## NOTES

1. STEVEN WALDMAN, THE BILL 236 (1995). Waldman's book is a study of the interactions between Congress and the new administration during legislative consideration of two bills: the law establishing a national service corps, and the law creating a federal direct educational loan program.

2. *Id.* At present, the "enormous gift" is taxable, but that aspect can and should be changed. See chapters 6 and 7.

3. In this book, I refer for convenience to the option as a "program," even though the government does not do so. The Department of Education regards income-contingent repayment as one formula among several others for paying back student loans, and the administration of direct lending and its repayment is the government's "program."

# 1

# Rising Costs and Rising Debt

## COSTS

For nearly fifteen years, observers of legal education have warned that the rapidly increasing cost of becoming a lawyer would eventually have deleterious effects on the profession. In 1987, John R. Kramer, then dean of Tulane Law School, noted that from 1974–75 to 1985–86 private law school tuition had increased from an average of $2,305 to an average of $8,286 (259 percent) and public law school tuition for in-state students had increased from $716 to $2,135 (198 percent). During this same period, the consumer price index had risen by only 120 percent.[1]

Kramer projected the trend forward to the year 2000, assuming three different rates of tuition increases: the 11.3 historical rate for private law schools, a more moderate 7 percent rate, and a "low" 5 percent rate. He assumed that students would continue to borrow at the same rate as in the past to pay for legal education. He concluded that "student borrowing would have to climb to at least $66,000 to cover the 73 percent of average private law school attendance costs (at the low predicted rate of inflation in tuition) now covered by the [federal guaranteed student] annual loan limit. . . . Because [the median] starting salary of $36,000 in 1982 will become $82,500 in 2003, assuming a 5 percent annual increase, a $66,000 debt might be barely affordable."[2] However, he noted, half the graduates would be earning less than the median.

The effect of these escalating costs and debt, Kramer worried, would be that law schools would be "filled with many more students who, as they became lawyers, do so with the single-minded objective of milking the profession for all it is worth in order to be able to pay retrospectively for their legal education."[3] Two years later, he noted that faced with continuing increases in the cost of legal education, some talented college graduates would give up their desire to become lawyers, and that students who did choose law school would "recoup their investment by ignoring the legal needs of four-fifths of the nation in order to service the one-fifth able to pay sizeable fees."[4] "How do you expand the range of career choice for graduating students saddled with tens of thousands of dollars of debt burden?" he asked. "Or do you simply tighten the corporate large firm practice noose around their necks and yank?"[5]

Professor David Chambers responded contemporaneously that "in some respects Kramer is not nearly gloomy enough."[6] He noted that Kramer failed to explore in any detail the situation of graduates who incurred the same law school expenses as everyone else but earned well below the median salary. Chambers feared that in the future "it may well become harder and harder to attract able beginning lawyers into government, legal services, and 'public interest' work."[7] Chambers had some empirical data to support his concern. A survey of Michigan Law School graduates showed that "nearly half of those with debts of $15,000 or more who were currently working in government, legal services, public defenders or other public interest settings reported that they had experienced moderate to great difficulty in meeting their obligations,"[8] and he predicted that with the cost of a legal education rising more quickly than inflation, "the starting lawyer with high debts will be substantially worse off in 1997 than in 1987."[9]

Kramer's 1987 predictions of the cost of attending a private law school in the year 2000 proved accurate.[10] By 1999, the average tuition at such a school had become nearly $21,000,[11] and the average annual cost of attendance (measured by tuition plus living expenses) had risen to $32,763.[12] Even by 1997, the cost of attendance at 50 of the nation's 180 law schools had exceeded $30,000 per year, and several schools were considerably more costly,[13] causing one scholar to observe that students entering some law schools in 2002 "will have to shoulder costs of attendance . . . of more than $155,000 for three years of schooling."[14] For students attending public law schools in their own states, in which legislative appropriations subsidized their education significantly, the 1999 cost was considerably less than at private law schools; students living off campus paid an average of only $18,415 for each of their three years.[15] However, tuition costs at such schools had been rising more quickly than at private law schools.[16]

## DEBT

Lending is the engine that makes it possible for students to attend law school.[17] Approximately 86 percent of law students borrow to pay for their education.[18] Students take out two types of loans: (1) they incur debt that is guaranteed by or extended by the federal government, and (2) they borrow commercially. Because it is less costly, they borrow first, to the extent permitted by law, through the federal Stafford loan program.[19] Government-guaranteed Stafford loans can be obtained from banks for undergraduate education, for legal education, or for both, through the Federal Family Education Loan Program (FFELP),[20] known in a pre-1992 incarnation as the federal guaranteed student loan program.[21] (At some universities, students may borrow directly from the federal government, through its federal direct lending program, rather than from banks).[22] Stafford loans are extended at lower rates than those of the commercial market, and they are subject to a statutory interest rate ceiling of 8.25 percent.[23] Only 1 percent of law students borrow for college but not for law school, whereas 53 percent borrow for law school only. Another 32 percent borrow for both levels of education.[24]

The Stafford loan program includes two types of loans. The first $8,500 per year that most law students borrow is subsidized,[25] in that the federal government pays the interest while the student is in school.[26] After borrowing $8,500 this way, a student may also borrow up to an additional $10,000 per year in unsubsidized Stafford loans.[27] As in the case of subsidized Stafford loans, the interest rate is linked annually to the rate for ninety-one-day Treasury bills,[28] but the maximum rate is 8.25 percent.[29] However, although a student may defer paying interest on the unsubsidized Stafford loan while in school, the unpaid interest is added to the principal (capitalized), so it will cause the size of the loan to increase.

Because the cost of attendance at many law schools exceeds the $18,500 that may be borrowed through Stafford loans, many students turn to private lenders to make up the difference. Typically, they turn to private lending programs that are specifically geared to law students, such as those offered by the Access Group, a major lender in this field. Because the loans are not government guaranteed, these programs charge higher rates of interest than the banks or the government charge on Stafford loans. However, some students do not qualify to receive sufficient credit from these private lending programs to cover all of their educational expenses. Some students are driven toward still more expensive private borrowing. For example, graduate students in the United States have an average of seven credit cards, and the average cumulative balance on

**Table 1.1**
**Cumulative Debt of Graduating Law Students**

| Year | Public Law Schools | | Private Law Schools | |
|------|--------------------|--------------------|--------------------|--------------------|
| | Average Federal Loan Debt | Average Total Debt | Average Federal Loan Debt | Average Total Debt |
| 1987–88 | — | — | — | $28,000 (est.) |
| 1992–93 | $22,278 | $28,945 | $30,887 | $41,776 |
| 1995–96 | $39,337 | $39,987 | $49,043 | $53,036 |
| 1999 (conservative estimate)[a] | $44,366 | $41,828 | $52,083 | $56,324 |

*Note*: The data from 1992–93 and 1995–96 were derived by Samuel M. Kipp III from the National Center for Education Statistics' National Postsecondary Student Aid Study 1992–93 and National Postsecondary Student Aid Study 1995–96 databases. See SAMUEL M. KIPP III, STUDENT BORROWING, DEBT BURDEN, AND DEFAULT: THE SPECIAL CASE OF FIRST-PROFESSIONAL STUDENTS IN THE 1990s at 21 (1998). They understate total indebtedness because they exclude credit card debt. Ibid. Good statistics are apparently unavailable before 1992–93. The 1988 estimate is based on an analysis of the cumulative debt ($22,000) of students graduating from Tulane Law School that year who had borrowed from Law Access, plus an estimated $6,000 of undergraduate debt with which they arrived in law school. Kramer, *Who Will Pay the Piper or Leave the Check on the Table for the Other Guy?*, 39 J. LEGAL EDUC. 655 (1989).
[a]This estimate was derived only by adjusting for 1996–99 inflation and assuming no real increase in borrowing, even though borrowing has historically outpaced inflation. U.S. government statistics show that average indebtedness for all 1997 first-professional (not only law) graduates was $66,200. NATIONAL CENTER FOR EDUCATION STATISTICS, DEBT BURDEN FOUR YEARS AFTER COLLEGE (NCES 2000–188) 56 (2000).

these cards is $5,800.[30] Credit card interest rates are often 16 percent to 18 percent per year.

In 1995–96, approximately one-quarter of all students at private law schools had private loans on top of their Stafford loans.[31] This percentage was bound to keep rising, at least until 2003, because whereas law school costs kept going up, the $18,500 annual limit on Stafford loans that was set by Congress in 1992 was not changed in the Congressional review of the Higher Education Act in 1997, and it is not scheduled for further legislative review until 2002–3.[32] When the annual Stafford limits are eventually increased, the amount of private lending may fall, but the amount of total borrowing will continue to increase.

The federal indebtedness and the total indebtedness of graduating law school students has increased steadily. Table 1.1 displays this increase.

From 1988 to 1996, the cost of living increased by 32.6 percent, so indebtedness of $28,000 in 1988 would amount (in 1996) to $37,128 in 1988 dollars. The 1995–96 $53,036 average total debt of private law school students therefore represents a considerable increase in terms of real dollars. Similarly, the 1992–93 average total private law school debt of $41,776 would have equated in 1996 to $45,368, not $53,036, if there had been no real increase.[33] From 1987 to 1999, the cost of living went up by less than 50 percent,[34] but the average debt of students graduating from private law schools doubled.

The $56,324 estimate of average debt (for students graduating from private law schools in 1999) is based on projections from data self-reported by students in a U.S. Department of Education survey, and it may significantly understate the amount of debt. Two recent studies suggest that the debt is actually higher. The National Association of Student Financial Aid Administrators' survey of financial aid administrators found that for law student borrowers graduating in 1998, average cumulative debt (including undergraduate debt) was $45,536 at public schools and $63,078 at private schools.[35] The Access Group, which probably extends the majority of loans to law students,[36] studied the average indebtedness of 1998 law graduates who had exhausted their three $18,500 Stafford loans and borrowed at least once from the Access Group. It found that the average indebtedness of these graduates was $79,852, not including accrued undergraduate debt.[37]

Averages can be misleading. Many schools have higher-than-average tuition or are located in regions in which the cost of living is particularly high. Also, within high-cost schools, students incur a range of debt, in part because some bring with them more family resources than others and some earn more during the summer. It is therefore worth noting that among law students graduating in 1995 from the 10 percent of law schools with the highest average indebtedness the average debt was $68,690.[38] Some law schools with a high average of indebtedness among graduating students in 1998 included California Western ($78,350), Catholic ($78,500), Georgetown ($82,600), George Washington ($80,050), Stetson ($91,897), Tulane ($96,596), and Whittier ($82,868).[39] The average law school debt (i.e., excluding college debt) of new George Washington students had increased from $30,000 to $71,000 in just eight years.[40]

Many law schools' average debt is lower than these very high figures, but even at schools with lower average debt, some students owe much more. Journalistic accounts report that some students graduating from law schools owe $90,000,[41] $100,000,[42] and $120,000.[43]

From one perspective, increasing law school costs and the concomitant debt that students incur are unproblematic, because the market will presumably respond appropriately. Consumers of legal service may pay more for it, making student loan repayment at least as easy in the future as it has been in the past. Alternatively, if consumers believe that legal service is overpriced (in part because legal education is too expensive), they will not pay more. Then some students will see that they cannot afford to become lawyers, and they will pursue other lines of education

**Table 1.2**
**Starting Salaries for Lawyers**

| Type of Practice | Median Starting Salary (Thousands of Dollars) | | Increase | 1999 Median Starting Salary (Thousands of 1993 Dollars) | Increase (Constant Dollars) |
|---|---|---|---|---|---|
| | 1993 | 1999 | | | |
| Private Practice | 48.0 | 70 | 46% | 60.7 | 27% |
| Business | 40.0 | 54 | 35% | 46.8 | 17% |
| Government | 31.6 | 38 | 20% | 32.9 | 4.4% |
| Public Interest | 27.0 | 32 | 18.5% | 27.7 | 2.6% |

*Note*: Data for the Class of 1993: National Association for Law Placement, Starting Salaries: What New Law Graduates Earn, Class of 1998 at 6 (1999). Data for the Class of 1999: National Association for Law Placement, Jobs and J.D.'s: Employment and Salaries of New Law Graduates, Class of 1999 at 18 (2000).

and employment. Society will have fewer lawyers, and some law schools might close, but those would be desirable consequences of market-based decisions to spend less on legal service.

Indeed, there is evidence that the market has been responding in the first of these ways, by paying lawyers more. Between 1993 and 1999, starting salaries in most sectors of the legal profession rose apace. (See Table 1.2.)

Thus, while the average cumulative debt at the nation's private law schools increased from $41,776 to $56,324 (35 percent in current dollars and 15 percent in constant dollars), starting salaries for lawyers in private practice and business surpassed the increase in accumulated debt. These two categories account for 69 percent of all new lawyers.[44]

The 26 percent real increase for lawyers in private practice may significantly understate the trend for this group, because a wave of major salary hikes in 1999–2000 apparently produced a further 20 percent increase, at least for lawyers starting at large corporate firms, just after these statistics were reported.[45] Among recent graduates who join private law firms, approximately 25 percent enter firms of more than 100 lawyers.[46]

Within these categories, some new lawyers at the turn of the 21st century were being paid at a rate far surpassing the median. Some new lawyers in the year 2000 started at salaries of $160,000 or more.[47]

The table also shows, however, that government lawyers (12.2 percent of beginning attorneys) and public interest lawyers (2.6 percent of such attorneys)[48] were falling behind the curve. Their real income increases of 4.4 percent and 2.6 percent did not keep up with the 15 percent real average indebtedness increase over the same period of time.[49] For them, the problem of debt is becoming more severe for each graduating class. It is not simply that the absolute amounts of debt are larger each year; that would not be a problem if salaries were keeping pace. For these graduates, debts are mounting more rapidly than starting salaries.

## THE PRESSURE ON PUBLIC INTEREST LAWYERS

How much pressure does this mounting debt actually put on new lawyers who seek public service jobs? An analysis of this problem must first take note of the prevalent idea that student loans should be paid within ten years after graduation. This concept is a psychological assumption on the part of most students. It is also very nearly a convention in the literature on debt repayment.

As all law student borrowers know, Stafford loans taken out through FFELP must be repaid within ten years, unless the borrower elects an alternative repayment plan.[50] This ten-year period is, according to the federal statute, the "standard repayment" period.[51] When the federal government lends money to students through the federal direct loan program, it offers other repayment options, but the direct federal lending program also calls ten-year repayment "standard repayment."[52] Students have become used to thinking of ten years as the "right" time within which to pay off student loans, even though, because of the existence of alternative repayment plans and subsequent consolidation opportunities, no student is required to do so.[53] Authorities on debt repayment also tend to treat ten-year repayment as standard, often not mentioning the alternatives.[54] The popular press read by law students reinforces the sanctity of a ten-year schedule. For example, in 1999, a dramatic cover story in *The National Jurist*, a magazine distributed free at law schools, concluded that average debt was so high at twenty-three law schools that graduates entering public practice would actually have a below-zero disposable income after making their loan payments. The magazine assumed that students would pay 1.3 percent of their debt per month, based on the empirical average paid by graduate students rather than the lowest amount that students could lawfully pay.[55] The ten-year term, more than any other factor, makes making ends meet on a low income very difficult.

Experts have offered certain benchmarks as measures of the dividing line between acceptable and excessive debt repayment. Reviewing the literature on debt manageability a decade ago, David Chambers noted that "the principal writers . . . hover within a fairly narrow range in their recommendations."[56] Andre L. Daniere, a leading authority, advised students not to incur indebtedness that would require them to pay more than 7.5 percent of net (after taxes) income, while Dwight Horch, another expert, suggested 9 percent for higher-income professionals.[57] John Kramer recommended 8 percent.[58] The U.S. Department of Education believes that the "median Federal [student] debt burden (yearly scheduled payments as a percentage of annual income of borrowers in their first year of repayment) [should] be less than 10 percent," because "as a general rule, it is believed that an educational debt burden of 10 percent or greater will negatively affect a student's ability to repay his or her student loan and obtain other credit such as a home mortgage."[59]

Over the years, however, single-digit percentages have been routinely exceeded by law graduates. Rather than lending less money or calling for subsidies, banking industry representatives have made ever-higher estimates of how much debt repayment is tolerable. In the early 1990s, they raised the level to about 15 percent, and later in the decade to 20 percent,[60] although as recently as 2000 some industry officials still recommended an 8 percent limit on gross income,[61] which works out, for a person earning $32,000, to about 9.4 percent of net income. However, *The National Jurist's* calculations (which understated the magnitude of the problem by erroneously excluding undergraduate debt)[62] showed that by 1998, seventy-one new law school graduates entering the public sector had debt-to-income ratios exceeding 20 percent.[63] Using the lower indebtedness figures from 1995, Samuel Kipp concluded that graduates with average debts and jobs paying the lowest decile of starting salaries would have to spend at least 26 percent of their already low incomes for ten-year debt repayment. Similar students with high debts would have to spend 36 percent of their incomes to pay back their student loans.[64] Lewis Kornhauser and Richard Revesz concluded that "an individual in these circumstances would accept a not-for-profit job only if she were independently wealthy, benefitted from generous [debt relief] assistance [from her law school], or could not secure more lucrative employment."[65]

These payment-to-salary ratios all assume ten-year repayment. However, as noted above, a law graduate could consolidate his or her loan and pay a lower amount each month. This procedure will, of course, stretch out the number of years during which he or she will have to pay. Furthermore, deferring payment of much of the debt will significantly increase the amount that has to be paid, because interest will accrue and compound for a longer period of time. The amount of additional payment will depend on the interest rate(s) applicable to the loan and the period of repayment. Table 1.3 assumes that a graduate is repaying $75,500, approximately the largest amount that he or she is likely to borrow through FFELP.[66] It assumes that the interest rate on the loan is 8.25 percent, the maximum that may be charged on Stafford loans. It shows the relationship between the duration of the loan term, the monthly payment, and the amount of actual dollars that the graduate

**Table 1.3**
**Cost of Repaying a $75,500 Loan at 8.25% Interest**

| Length of Repayment (Years) | Monthly Payments | Annual Payment | Total Actual Payments (Rounded to Nearest Thousand) | Present Value of All Payments (Rounded to Nearest Thousand) |
|---|---|---|---|---|
| 10 | $926 | $11,112 | $111,000 | $83,000 |
| 15 | $732 | $8,789 | $132,000 | $87,000 |
| 20 | $643 | $7,720 | $154,000 | $90,000 |
| 25 | $595 | $7,143 | $179,000 | $92,000 |
| 30 | $567 | $6,806 | $204,000 | $95,000 |

will eventually have to pay. It also includes a column showing the value in current dollars of the total repayment, an amount much smaller than the actual dollar cost of repayment because a dollar that must be paid to a creditor after twenty years of inflation is much less valuable than a dollar that is paid immediately. The table discounts the value of money by 5.8 percent per annum, the rate of interest as of September 14, 2000, on thirty-year U.S. treasury bonds.[67]

The table shows that stretching out a debt from ten years to a much longer period of repayment does reduce the monthly repayment significantly, and that, of course, the total amount that must be repaid increases greatly. It also shows that measured in terms of the present value of future payments, the increase in the cost of repayment is not nearly as dramatic as the straight dollar comparison suggests. The fact that they are paying in dollars worth less than in yesteryear may seem cold comfort to students who are actually repaying $200,000 for a $75,000 loan, but as John Kramer noted long ago, "the total amount of dollars exacted by the penalty [of paying over a longer period] may overstate the actual burden on the graduate."[68]

As noted above, students at some major private law schools graduate with debts considerably higher than $75,500. Because they are unable to borrow more than $18,500 in government-guaranteed loans, they must borrow the additional funds commercially. Table 1.4 shows the additional cost of repaying $30,000 in commercial loans. The interest rate on such loans is not capped at 8.25 percent. In June 2000, students fortunate enough to obtain a relatively good rate would pay approximately 8.64 percent, and that is the rate used in this table.[69]

A lawyer who graduates owing $105,500 would combine those figures shown by Tables 1.3 and 1.4, as indicated in Table 1.5.

A graduate who owes about $105,000 could therefore reduce the annual payment from about $15,600 to about $9,600 (a 38.5 percent reduc-

**Table 1.4**
**Cost of Repaying $30,000 Borrowed Commercially at 8.64%**

| Length of Repayment (Years) | Monthly Payments | Annual Payment | Total Actual Payments (Rounded to Nearest Thousand) | Present Value of All Payments (Rounded to Nearest Thousand) |
|---|---|---|---|---|
| 10 | $374 | $4,488 | $45,000 | $34,000 |
| 15 | $298 | $3,572 | $54,000 | $36,000 |
| 20 | $263 | $3,154 | $63,000 | $37,000 |
| 25 | $244 | $2,930 | $73,000 | $38,000 |
| 30 | $233 | $2,801 | $84,000 | $39,000 |

**Table 1.5**
**Repayments Required of a Typical Graduate Owing $105,500**

| Length of Repayment (Years) | Monthly Payments | Annual Payment | Total Actual Payments (Rounded to Nearest Thousand) | Present Value of All Payments (Rounded to Nearest Thousand) |
|---|---|---|---|---|
| 10 | $1,300 | $15,600 | $156,000 | $117,000 |
| 15 | $1,030 | $12,361 | $186,000 | $123,000 |
| 20 | $906 | $10,874 | $217,000 | $127,000 |
| 25 | $839 | $10,073 | $252,000 | $130,000 |
| 30 | $800 | $9,607 | $288,000 | $134,000 |

tion) by stretching out the payments over thirty years and by agreeing to repay a total of $288,000 rather than $156,000 (an 84.6 percent increase measured in current dollars, though only about 15 percent more in constant dollars if a 5.8 percent discount rate is used). However, even stretched out, loans that lower current payments by 38.5 percent are not affordable for public interest lawyers. Recall that the median 1999 starting salary for public interest lawyers was $32,000. Federal tax on that amount for a single filer was $3,784;[70] taking into account state and local tax, the graduate's after-tax income would be about $27,000. Even the most stretched out repayment of $9,607 annually would require the graduate to pay 36 percent of after-tax income toward the student debt, far in excess of even the highest figure (20 percent) recommended by a banking official. Furthermore, that stretched-out repayment would require the graduate, over thirty years, to write checks for $288,000 to repay the $105,500 student loan.

## THE CASE FOR A SUBSIDY

If stretching out loans is not sufficient to enable law graduates to become public interest lawyers, perhaps public or private subsidies should be encouraged. Before considering the effect of the subsidies that are built into the income-contingent repayment option, however, it is worth taking a moment to return to the idea that if there is a problem here, the market will solve it. The market for corporate legal services already appears to be adjusting to the high cost of education.[71] If salaries for public interest lawyers are too low to enable them to repay their educational debts, perhaps the market is signaling that we have an oversupply of government and public interest lawyers. In this view, the trend in which debt is rising faster than income for public interest lawyers is at worst a temporary problem that will eventually vanish as new lawyers simply reject the less remunerative nonprofit specialties and join the ranks of the corporate world.

From a different perspective, however, governmental or public interest legal services might be regarded as a public good deserving of a subsidy because the market does not value them highly enough.[72] The nation provides many kinds of subsidized services, including some legal services, to its least fortunate residents. Furthermore, a nation that in the short run would rather have more corporate and fewer public interest lawyers may want to pay a modest sum to preserve the strain of idealism and the culture of public service embodied by public interest lawyers and the students who become such lawyers.

A glimpse at what would happen if students who want to become public interest lawyers are not sufficiently subsidized may clarify the cost of treating the market-driven status quo as good enough. We may perceive several effects that some, including the author, regard as unfortunate.

### Effects on Nonprofit Public Service Institutions and Their Clients

It is well known that the civil legal needs of the nation's poor are not being met. Attorney General Janet Reno reminded the nation in 1994 that "eighty to ninety percent of the poor and working poor in America do not have access to legal services."[73] Her conclusion is supported by several academic studies.[74] Legal aid organizations obviously need more public support, either directly through larger federal grants or indirectly through loan repayment subsidies that enable them to spread their scarce payroll dollars among more lawyers. As lawyers' debt burdens rise, fewer graduates will be able to afford to work in poorly paid public interest jobs that serve the poor and near-poor. In the short run, public interest organizations such as legal services offices, public defender organizations, and local governments may still be able to fill vacancies, but expansion will be limited. At present, many law students are idealistic and would like to engage in public service,[75] and most nonprofit organizations currently have little trouble attracting applicants for the few jobs that become available.[76] However, to the extent that students at high-cost law schools are unable to consider such employment because the low salaries are insufficient to enable them to repay their loans, these organizations cannot participate in a truly national labor market. In time, their recruiting will be limited to the small proportion of lawyers who are independently wealthy, lawyers who went to state law schools where their educations were subsidized by state taxpayers, and graduates of the minority of law schools (possibly as few as six such schools) that pay generous subsidies through their own loan repayment programs to graduates who perform public service.[77]

Furthermore, the world does not have a static number of public service jobs. The number and variety of such positions expand in part because law students and young lawyers who want to work in such organizations create new positions. Some win "seed money" foundation grants to establish new organizations through which they will be employed.[78] Others volunteer with organizations and become so indispensable that the organizations intensify fund-raising efforts to retain them. As debt closes off the opportunity to establish new low-income positions, this pie-expanding phenomenon will be curtailed.

To the extent that increasing indebtedness precludes lawyers from accepting full-time public service employment, the gap might in principle be filled by an increased commitment from law firms to encourage pro bono work by their lawyers. Unfortunately, the world seems to be moving in the opposite direction. As salaries for lawyers have skyrocketed in recent years (reducing partners' profits), the subtle pressure on many firms' associates not to contribute pro bono time has intensified.[79] Lawyers at the 100 top American law firms are now expected to bill for 2,200 hours per year compared to 1,700 a few years ago, and in 1999, even before the major salary increases that took effect in 2000, they spent only thirty-six hours per year doing pro bono work, compared to fifty-six hours in 1992.[80]

## Effects on Individual and Family Consumers of Legal Services

As costs and debts rise, not only the very poor (who are often served through nonprofit organizations) but also ordinary families and workers are relegated to an ever-constricting legal market. Like the poor, they will be unable to obtain legal representation[81] or will have to choose among a limited pool of lawyers who for personal reasons are not forced by their debts to work for wealthy corporations. Some law students would like to spend their careers representing ordinary Americans with routine legal problems; they seek neither a practice in which they will serve large corporations and their wealthy executives nor the very poor. However, the solo practitioners and small firms who have long been the nation's family lawyers are able to pay far less than the large corporate firms. For 1999 graduates, the median starting salary in firms employing two to ten lawyers was $40,000, compared with $97,000 for firms with more than 500 lawyers and $92,000 in firms with 251 to 500 lawyers.[82] If public interest lawyers are driven out of the labor market by rising costs, small firm lawyers may not be far behind.

## Effects on Law School and Legal Culture

Already, lawyers are perceived as wealthy and greedy, an image re-flected in thousands of jokes but mitigated in part by frequent news stories of public service lawyers who selflessly serve poor people, death penalty defendants, rejected minorities, and unpopular causes. The pro-fession, the community of law students headed for business careers, and the nation would experience a loss if this segment of lawyers and law students were to disappear in favor of more mercenary recruits.

## Effects on Law Students

The extinction of law students who want to become public servants would not occur in one or two years. As the gap between debt and income continues to grow, law students contemplating careers in public service would continue to struggle to live up to their ideals, but life would become increasingly unpleasant for them. Already, some new graduates who have chosen the nonprofit sector are finding the struggle to repay student loans exceedingly difficult. For example, Stacey Klein, a 1998 Stetson graduate earning $25,000 as a legal services lawyer in Tampa, had to take a part-time job as a waitress to make ends meet.[83] Marie Tatro, earning $34,000 at Brooklyn Legal Services, owned no skirts and one pair of black pants for court appearances and counted on birth-day gifts for clothing.[84] Leonard Adler, $100,000 in debt and living on $30,000 that had to cover both his personal expenses and those of his new National Anti-Poverty Organization, lived in an attic with no heat-ing and spent only $100 a month on food.[85] In general, students responding to a 1997 survey were much more likely than those responding to the same survey in 1991 to report that student debts had interfered with major life choices such as having children,[86] although even in 1997 it appeared that students as a whole (as opposed to the much smaller group of high-debt, low-income law graduates)[87] had not changed their lifestyle because of debt as much as they believed they had.[88] Consider the subgroup of borrowers in that survey whose payments exceed 10 percent of their incomes. This subgroup (only 18 percent of which were law graduates) was much more fortunate than the high-debt borrowers now graduating from American law schools. Its median total debt was only $32,500. Nevertheless, it reported that the debt impacted significantly on lifestyle. For example, 57 percent of these borrowers reported that their ·debts had delayed home purchasing (compared with 38 percent with lower payment-to-income ratios), 28 percent reported that debts had delayed moving out of their parents' homes (compared with 12 percent), and 33 percent reported that debts had delayed having children (compared with 19 percent).[89]

Furthermore, many idealistic students do not realize before choosing law as a career that they may have to borrow more than $100,000 or that starting salaries for public interest lawyers are so low that they will have trouble repaying sums at this level. Law schools and faculty members are understandably reluctant to advise new students to abandon their goals or their career aspirations. Accordingly, when students realize partway through law school the extent of the financial pressure on them to join corporate law firms,[90] they often become resentful or embittered. This phenomenon will increase unless law schools become more forceful in advertising themselves only as trade schools for business lawyers (except, of course, for those students who are so wealthy that they do not need to borrow).

Finally, to the extent that students insist on sticking to their career plans, the default rate is certain to increase. Defaults will affect the credit histories of the law graduates. In addition, more defaults will increase the cost to the taxpayers who guarantee student loans and cause rate increases or loan denials for future students.[91] Already, the default rate is at least 15 percent on the commercial loans that law students take when they exhaust the $18,500 per year of government-guaranteed loans that are available to them.[92]

This description of the costs of allowing the rate at which indebtedness rises to exceed the rate at which income rises may not convince everyone that public interest lawyers, or low-income practitioners who serve individuals and families rather than businesses, should be subsidized. Appreciation of market inefficiencies[93] may help to justify government intervention, but the key difference between those who might support a subsidy and those who are less likely to do so is a difference of values.

Supporters of subsidies are likely to agree that taxpayers should take more responsibility to assist the less fortunate in a nation in which the gap between the rich and the poor is very great and continues to become larger each decade[94] and that those who cannot pay their own way in their effort to secure justice should be served by public interest lawyers.[95] The author is among those who believe that at least for the present time, some degree of subsidy is warranted, but the author's personal opinion is not particularly important. The nation as a whole has already addressed the basic question of subsidization for high-debt, low-income graduates, particularly those who desire public service. On this very point, Congress has acted.[96]

## NOTES

1. John R. Kramer, *Will Legal Education Remain Affordable, by Whom, and How?*, 1987 DUKE L.J. 240, 242–43 (1987).

2. *Id.* at 267.

3. *Id.* at 240–41.

4. John R. Kramer, *Who Will Pay the Piper or Leave the Check on the Table for the Other Guy?* 39 J. LEGAL EDUC. 655 (1989).

5. *Id.* at 671.

6. David L. Chambers, *Educational Debts and the Worsening Position of Small-Firm, Government, and Legal-Services Lawyers*, 39 J. LEGAL EDUC. 709 (1989).

7. *Id.* at 710.

8. *Id.* at 719.

9. *Id.* at 722.

10. Kramer predicted an annual 2000–2001 cost of attendance for private law school in the range of $29,000 to $55,000. *See* Kramer, *Will Legal Education Remain Affordable?, supra* note 1, at 245. He put the cost of public law school attendance in the $16,000 to $20,000 range.  .

11. The precise private school tuition average was $20,709. E-mail from Rick Morgan, American Bar Association, to the author (June 13, 2000) (on file with author). *See also* Michael A. Olivas, *Paying for a Law Degree: Trends in Student Borrowing and the Ability to Repay Debt*, 49 J. LEGAL EDUC. 333 (1999) (published figures for 1975 and 1997). Olivas (who is the William B. Bates Professor of Law at the University of Houston) is a trustee of the Access Group, a major private lender, and his data were supplied by Access Group. *Id.* at note 1. From 1997–98 to 1998–99, tuition at ABA-approved law schools increased 6 percent, compared to a national inflation rate of 1.6 percent.

12. Morgan, *supra* note 11 (cost of living off campus while law school for a year is an additional $12,054, public and private law schools com-

bined). By another measure, which counts into the cost of legal education the lost wages that the student could have earned while attending law school, the cost of attendance is considerably greater. Kramer, *Will Legal Education Remain Affordable?, supra* note 1, at 247.

13. Olivas, *supra* note 11, at 334.

14. Ibid.

15. Morgan, *supra* note 11 (1999 public law school tuition for in-state residents and off-campus living expenses).

16. Average public law school tuition for in-state residents rose from $780 to $6,000 between 1975 and 1997. Olivas, *supra* note 11, at 333. Average in-state tuition rose another 6 percent in 1998 and a further 6 percent in 1999. Morgan, *supra* note 11.

17. Some students receive money from parents for law school attendance, but even in 1987, John Kramer could write that most students "are given either more than $10,000 or nothing at all" and that the emergence of a large federal lending program was encouraging parents "to abandon a previously accepted responsibility," causing students to have to find money for legal education themselves. Kramer, *Will Legal Education Remain Affordable?, supra* note 1, at 252.

18. Eighty-six percent of lawyers graduating in 1996 had borrowed. An increasingly high percentage borrow as the cost of attendance rises; the corresponding percentage for the class of 1993 was 81 percent. SAMUEL M. KIPP, III, STUDENT BORROWING, DEBT BURDEN, AND DEFAULT: THE SPECIAL CASE OF FIRST-PROFESSIONAL STUDENTS IN THE 1990s at 25 (1998).

19. 20 U.S.C. §§ 1078, 1078–8 (2000). Students with exceptional financial need may also borrow up to $6,000 per year (for graduate students) through the Perkins Loan Program, in which the interest rate is capped at 5 percent. 20 U.S.C. § 1087dd (2000). *See also* ANNE STOCKWELL, THE GUERRILLA GUIDE TO MASTERING STUDENT LOAN DEBT (1997). This manual, written for students, is a well-known introductory orientation to the institutions that manage student loan programs. It contains much useful history of federal financial aid, and it offers considerable help with terminology and concepts. However, it does not describe repayment plans in detail.

20. 20 U.S.C. § 1071 (2000) et. seq.

21. See STOCKWELL, *supra* note 19, at 59.

22. 20 U.S.C. § 1087a (2000).

23. 20 U.S.C. §§ 1077(a) (2000) (original loans); 1087(e) (2000) (consolidation loans).

24. KIPP, *supra* note 18, at 25.

25. Eligibility rules for subsidized Stafford loans to law students are sufficiently generous that an estimated 95 percent to 97 percent of the Georgetown University law students who borrow receive subsidized Stafford funds. E-mail from Ruth Lammert-Reeves, assistant dean for

financial aid, Georgetown University Law Center, to the author (July 21, 2000) (on file with author).

26. 20 U.S.C. § 1077a(k) (2000).

27. 20 U.S.C. § 1078–8 (2000). If the student is not eligible to borrow the full $8,500 in subsidized Stafford funds, he or she may borrow that money as part of the unsubsidized Stafford loan. Ibid.

28. The rate is 1.7 percent more than the ninety-one-day rate for the previous May while the borrower is in school and for a short time thereafter, and 2.3 percent above that rate for the duration of repayment. 20 U.S.C. § 1077a(k) (2000). For loans that are consolidated, the interest rate becomes fixed; it is the weighted average of the rate being paid for each of the consolidated loans at the time they are consolidated, rounded up to the nearest higher ⅛ of 1 percent, with a cap of 8.25 percent. 20 U.S.C. § 1077a(k)(4) (2000).

29. 20 U.S.C. §§ 1078–8(e)(4), 1077a(k)(1) (2000).

30. Comment of Diane Saunders, vice president of Communications and Public Affairs, Nellie Mae, *in* ACCESS GROUP, SYMPOSIUM ON HIGHER EDUCATION FINANCING, CRITICAL CHALLENGES IN FINANCING GRADUATE AND PROFESSIONAL DEGREES 57(1997). Nine percent of graduate students have credit card balances exceeding $15,000. Ibid.

31. KIPP, *supra* note 18, at 22, table 4.

32. The percentage of law students borrowing from private sources fell (from 36 percent) after 1992, because in that year Congress raised the loan limit to $18,500 and made eligibility criteria much more generous. "[M]ore than 60 percent of the increase in cumulative federal borrowing . . . was actually the result of substituting lower-cost federal loans for private loans." KIPP, *supra* note 18, at 21.

33. Unless otherwise stated, inflation adjustments in this book were computed using the National Aeronautical and Space Agency's Consumer Price Index Inflation Calculator, http://www.jsc.nasa.gov/bu2/inflateCPI.html.

34. The increase over these years was 46.7 percent.

35. Kenneth E. Redd, *Policies, Practices, and Procedures in Graduate Student Aid: A Report on the 1998 NASFAA SOGAPPP Survey*, NASFAA's STUDENT AID TRANSCRIPT 10, 18 (Spring 2000).

36. Telephone interview with Jeff Hanson, Access Group analyst (June 29, 2000). Law students probably know this lender by the term Law Access, its division for law school lending.

37. Access Update, "The Price of Law School: An Access Group Analysis" (Mar. 2000), http://www.accessgroup.org/update/3_2000/5.htm (last visited June 27, 2000). The components of the indebtedness were: subsidized Stafford loan borrowed, $25,500; principal amount of unsubsidized Stafford loan, $30,000; accrued interest on unsubsidized Stafford loan (at 8.25 percent per annum), $5,259; principal amount of private

loan, $14,000; accrued interest on private loan (at 8.76 percent per annum), $2,911; guarantee fee (covers defaults on private loans) due at repayment, $2,181. Memorandum from Jeff Hanson, Access Group, to interested parties on Average Debt at Repayment, Law School Class of 1998—Revised (Jan. 26, 2000) (on file with author).

38. KIPP, *supra* note 18, at 29.

39. These figures were derived from reports of average 1998 graduating debt supplied by law schools to *U.S. News and World Report* and compiled on its website, http://www.usnews.com/utils/gradlaw. The figures reported here are $9,500 higher than those listed on the website, because the magazine requested from law schools only the average debt resulting from law school loans; the data thus excludes outstanding college debt. E-mail from Georgetown's financial aid director, Ruth Lammert-Reeves, to the author (June 12, 2000) (on file with author). The excluded outstanding educational debt from undergraduate studies was $9,546. Lawopoly Clarification, www.natjurist.com/meath.shtml, downloaded from the website of the magazine *The National Jurist* (Mar. 2, 1999). The *Jurist*'s data were based on U.S. Department of Education statistics. For the class of 1999, the average cumulative debt at Georgetown had grown by an additional $5,920, so for that class it was approximately $88,520 (after a $9,500 upward adjustment for college debt). E-mail from Ruth Lammert-Reeves, *supra*.

40. Kate Ackley, *Til Debt Do Us Part*, LEGAL TIMES, Sept. 6, 1999, at 30, 31; Ginny Edwards, *Making Public Interest Law Interesting*, PUBLIC LAWYER, Winter 1999, at 6. I do not mean to suggest that the average distribution of student indebtedness among institutions deviates from the usual bell curve, but only that policy makers should be concerned, perhaps especially concerned, about those at the high end as well as other parts of the curve.

41. Alia Malek, Georgetown University Law Center, 1999, *in* Ackley, *supra* note, 40, at S30.

42. Leonard Adler, Georgetown University Law Center 1994, *in Financial Aid*, NAT'L JURIST ON LINE, Apr.–May 1998.

43. Greta Hinkle, American University Law School class of 1999, *in* Tom Stabile, *Lawopoly: Borrowed Time (Part 2 of 2)*, NAT'L JURIST, April 1999, at 14. Bennett Miller, chair of the American Bar Association's student division in 1999, knew of one couple who had graduated from Northwestern University law school owing a combined $250,000. Mark Hansen, *And Debt's All, Folks*, ABA JOURNAL, June 1999, at 24.

44. NAT'L ASS'N FOR LAW PLACEMENT, JOBS AND J.D.'S: EMPLOYMENT AND SALARIES OF NEW LAW GRADUATES, CLASS OF 1998 at 13 (1999).

45. David Phelps, *Not Just Pocket Change: Local Law School Graduates Will Land Average Starting Salaries of $66,000 This Year, up 20 Percent from a Year Ago*, MINN. STAR-TRIB., Apr. 23, 2000, at 1D; Jeffrey McCracken,

*Boom Fuels Lawyer Pay Surge*, CRAIN'S DETROIT BUS., Apr. 10, 2000, at 3 (Detroit firms raising starting pay by $20,000 to $35,000 in 2000, compared to $3,500 in 1999); Jessica Guynn, *For Bay Area Attorneys, Salaries in Stratosphere*, CONTRA COSTA TIMES, Feb. 19, 2000 (average large-firm starting salaries increased to $125,000, with some firms offering $165,000); David Leonhardt, *Law Firms' Pay Soars to Stem Dot-Com Defections*, N.Y. TIMES, Feb. 2, 2000, at 1 (top New York firms raising starting pay to $160,000, and firms around the country were expected to follow with significant raises).

46. NAT'L ASS'N FOR LAW PLACEMENT, *supra* note 44, at 28.

47. David Leonhardt, *supra* note 45, at 1.

48. NAT'L ASS'N FOR LAW PLACEMENT, *supra* note 44, at 13.

49. A Department of Education official who read an earlier draft of this book, including the statistics reported in the table of starting salaries, wrote to the author that the numbers reported by the National Association for Law Placement for starting and mid-career salaries of government officials "seems erroneously high, particularly based on all the letters my office received from low-paid public defenders and prosecutors earlier this year." E-mail from a Department of Education official to the author (Aug. 1, 2000) (on file with the author).

50. 20 U.S.C. § 1078(b)(9)(B) (2000). Students receive this information in written form from their financial aid offices, from the lenders who handle their loan, or from websites such as Law Access, http://www. accessgroup.org/loan_terms/FedLoan/Fedgrad.htm?Template=Fedgra dInfo2000.htm&SchoolId=143700&Location=http://www.accessgroup. org/loan_terms/contents.htm&AppReferrer= (last visited June 13, 2000) (Stafford loan information, "up to ten years to repay . . . Flexible repayment options and federal loan consolidation also available").

51. 20 U.S.C. § 1078(b)(9)(A)(i) (2000).

52. 20 U.S.C. §§ 1087e(d)(1)(A), 1087e (a)(1) (2000)).

53. *See* 20 U.S.C. § 1078(b)(9)(A) (other repayment plans), 20 U.S.C. §§ 1087e(d), (g) (2000) (students may consolidate government-guaranteed loans such as Stafford loans into a federal direct loan with a longer repayment term). Private loans typically offer repayment terms longer than ten years. *See, e.g.,* Law Access Loans, described at www.accessgroup.org (follow clicks to Law Access Loan Terms).

54. For example, Olivas uses a ten-year repayment table to compute the "monthly payment" for various types of graduate students who owe average debts, without identifying that he is doing so. Olivas, *supra* note 11, at 338. In his discussion of law graduate debt repayment, Kipp also treats only ten-year repayment, stating that "if they had medium or high debt levels, those on the lowest end of the salary scale would require 26 percent or more of their gross monthly earnings to repay their student loans within ten years." KIPP, *supra* note 18, at 30. Kipp does not explore

longer repayment options. Kornhauser and Revesz analyze debt burdens by reference to both ten-year and fifteen-year repayment schedules, but they do not consider longer repayment terms. Lewis A. Kornhauser & Richard L. Revesz, *Legal Education and Entry into the Legal Profession: The Role of Race, Gender and Educational Debt*, 70 N.Y.U.L.REV. 829, 890 (1995).

55. Jack Crittenden, *Lawopoly, Part 1 of 2*, NAT'L JURIST, Feb. 1999, at 17–18.

56. David Chambers, *supra* note 6, at 717.

57. Ibid.

58. Kramer, *Will Legal Education Remain Affordable?*, *supra* note 1, at 263.

59. U.S. Department of Education, Student Financial Assistance Policy, Indicator 1.4, http://www.ed.gov/pubs/AnnualPlan 2001/069-red.pdf (last visited Sept. 5, 2000).

60. Crittenden, *supra* note. 55, at 15 (quoting Diane Saunders, vice president of Communications and Public Affairs at Nellie Mae, a major lender).

61. USA GROUP FOUNDATION, STUDENT DEBT LEVELS CONTINUE TO RISE, STAFFORD INDEBTEDNESS: 1999 UPDATE 7 (2000). ("Lenders frequently recommend that borrowers limit their monthly student loan payments to no more than 8 percent of their pre-tax monthly incomes. Although arbitrary, this guideline helps ensure that monthly installments remain a manageable share of household budgets.")

62. "A clarification," *supra* note 39.

63. Crittenden, *supra* note 55, at 15.

64. KIPP, *supra* note 18, at 30, table 9.

65. Kornhauser & Revesz, *supra* note 54, at 890. Law school debt repayment assistance plans are discussed in chapter 5. Kornhauser and Revesz erroneously believed that they "are now becoming commonplace and quite generous." Ibid. However, by 1999, only 47 law schools of the 182 law schools accredited by the American Bar Association had such plans, and they varied considerably in the generosity of their benefits. In fact, just six law schools disbursed 70 percent of all of the benefits offered by the forty-seven loan repayment programs. NAT'L ASS'N FOR PUBLIC INTEREST LAW, FINANCING THE FUTURE: NAPIL'S 2000 REPORT ON LAW SCHOOL LOAN REPAYMENT ASSISTANCE AND PUBLIC INTEREST SCHOLARSHIP PROGRAMS 10 (2000).

66. This assumes approximately $55,500 in law student Stafford loans, $5,000 in accrued interest, and $15,000 in undergraduate debt. In 1996, the average undergraduate debt for law students was between $9,000 and $10,000, although the average undergraduate debt for graduates of four-year private colleges was $14,290. KIPP, *supra* note 18, at 25, 35. The average undergraduate debt for law students had been falling slightly, perhaps because those with already high debt levels were less likely to

continue on to law school. See KIPP, *supra* note 18, at 40. This book uses many examples that assume an accumulated undergraduate debt of $15,000, in part to adjust the 1996 figures for inflation and in part because I am concerned not only with the average student but also with students (such as graduates from four-year private colleges) whose debts are greater than average (and whose incomes are significantly below average).

67. Because a dollar repaid in the future is less valuable than a dollar that is repaid at once, discounting the stream of future loan repayments to present value (i.e., to constant dollars) is important. However, selecting the appropriate discount rate for future loan repayments is not simple. The thirty-year treasury bond rate seems a conservative choice, and the tables in this book use a discount rate of 5.8 percent, the thirty-year bond rate in September 2000. An appendix to this book discusses the issue of discounting and the reasons for choosing the thirty-year bond rate. The income-contingent repayment calculator at www.finaid.org uses the thirty-year bond rate as its default value but allows the user to select any other rate.

68. Kramer, *Will Legal Education Remain Affordable?*, *supra* note 1, at 267.

69. The rates vary slightly by offerer and school of attendance. This is the Law Access Loan offered by the Access Group to Georgetown University law students. This company offers a rate of 2.75 percent above the ninety-one-day treasury bill rate, which was 5.885 percent for the second quarter of calendar year 2000. The rate is actually understated, because Law Access also requires a one-time payment of at least an additional 6.9 percent of the amount borrowed as a "guarantee fee," to be paid just before the last payment is made. Information provided at the Law Access website, www.accessgroup.org (last visited June 13, 2000). Significantly higher rates are imposed on students at other schools. See chapter 7, note 38.

70. This calculation assumes that the taxpayer would take the standard deduction of $4,150 and had a personal exemption of $2,650. The tax is based on 1999 federal tax tables, at http://www.irs.gov/prod/ind_info/tax_tables/tbl_035k.html (last visited June 21, 2000).

71. *See* Table 2.

72. In recent years, programs of law school subsidies for students who want to become public interest lawyers have grown dramatically. *See* NAT'L ASS'N FOR PUBLIC INTEREST LAW, *supra* note 65, at 17 (subsidy growth from $3 million in 1993–94 to 7.5 million, given out through forty-seven law school programs, in 1998–99). This development suggests that within the community of legal educators, there is broad agreement that such subsidies are desirable. Not everyone agrees with this view, however, either inside or outside the law school community.

Nevertheless, even a very strong free market advocate who disapproves of subsidies for public interest lawyers, particularly those serving ideological communities because "there is no guarantee that gains in utility will exceed losses in utility and result in an overall increase in societal welfare," recognizes that "there appears to be a consensus . . . that there is substantial unmet need for civil poverty lawyers and that criminal representation is barely adequate [so a] law school may conclude that both the immediate donees and the public at large would benefit if the law school were to make a charitable contribution that increased legal services for the poor." Luize E. Zubrow, *Is Loan Forgiveness Divine? Another View*, 59 Geo. Wash. L. Rev. 451, 513–15 (1991).

73. Janet Reno, address delivered at the Celebration of the Seventy-Fifth Anniversary of Women at Fordham Law School, *in* 63 Fordham L. Rev. 5, 12 (1994).

74. *See, e.g.*, Family Law Section, Committee on the Probate and Family Court, Massachusetts Bar Association, Changing the Culture of the Probate and Family Court 26 (1997) (in probate and family court, at least one party is unrepresented in approximately 80 percent of cases); William P. Quigley, *The Unmet Civil Legal Needs of the Poor in Louisiana*, 19 S.U.L. Rev. 273 (1992) (85 percent to 92 percent of the low-income people in Louisiana who had civil legal needs in 1991 were unrepresented); Advisory Council on Family Legal Needs of Low Income Persons, Increasing Access to Justice for Maryland's Families (1992) (only 11 percent of Maryland's poor who have domestic problems receive legal assistance); Jane C. Murphy, *Access to Legal Remedies: The Crisis in Family Law*, 8 B.Y.U.J. Pub. L. 123 (1993) (summary of several surveys).

75. In 1998, in a survey of 548 entering first-year law students conducted by Georgetown University Law Center, 20 percent of the respondents said that "public interest" work best described their current plans for using their law degrees. Another 16 percent selected "government practice." Georgetown University Law Center, 1998 Survey of Entering Students (Sept. 17, 1998). These percentages are slightly overstated, as students were allowed to select more than one career option, and the total of the percentages selected by all students was therefore 108 percent rather than 100 percent.

76. Even now, this generalization is not universally true. In 1993, a survey by the Legal Services Corporation found that 57 percent of Legal Services Corporation field program directors had difficulty recruiting attorneys, and 55 percent reported educational debt as a constraint on the number of applications. Nat'l Ass'n for Public Interest Law, Comments on Proposed Regulations, Corporation for National and Community Service Grant Programs and Support for Investment Activities 3 (1994). Some other public interest organizations also expe-

rience recruiting difficulty. The American Bar Association operates Probar, a highly reputed office serving the needs of aliens who need legal representation at the border in Harlingen, Texas. The Association began advertising in October 1999, for a lawyer with two years' immigration experience to serve in the Probar office, and the position was still unfilled in June 2000. E-mail from Carol Wolchok, American Bar Association staff member, to the author (June 12, 2000) (on file with author).

77. See supra note 65.

78. For example, the Vanguard Public Foundation (which contributed $5,000) and the Echoing Green Foundation (which provided $25,000) made it possible for Van Jones to start the Ella Baker Center for Human Rights in San Francisco. Rinat Fried, *Civil Rights Lawyer Fights Police Conduct*, RECORDER, Sept. 11, 1995, at 2. Three years later, Mr. Jones had succeeded in forcing the dismissal from the police force of an officer who had killed two suspects, and he won the Reebok International Human Rights Award. Susan Gray, *Lawyer's Fight against Rogue Cop Becomes Crusade for Human Rights*, CHRON. OF PHILANTHROPY, Jan. 14, 1999. The echoing green Foundation also provided a small grant to enable Eric Rosenthal to start Mental Disability Rights International, now a well-respected human rights organization. *See* Stacy Weiner, *Speaking Up for the Mentally Disabled: Eric Rosenthal Brings Their Plight to the World*, WASH. POST, Jan. 18, 2000, at C1.

79. Some firms remain strongly committed to a pro bono tradition and count pro bono time toward an associate's billable hours, in a few cases not even distinguishing the purpose of the hours spent in reports that go to the partners, but such firms appear to be a minority.

80. Greg Winter, *Legal Firms Cutting Back on Free Services for Poor*, N.Y. TIMES, Aug. 17, 2000, at 1.

81. It could be argued that society should expect a family with modest resources to choose to spend even a high proportion of those resources on expensive legal services, if it needs a lawyer, and to forego alternative spending, but that analysis treats legal services as just another consumption choice like buying a car or taking a vacation. Frank Michelman has argued effectively that the right to counsel, particularly for purposes of litigation, involves considerations not applicable to ordinary consumer goods and services. These include concerns about individual dignity when judicial redress is needed, the citizen's political or governmental participation that is implicit in litigation, the ways in which individual litigation affects the rights of others in society (e.g., by deterring civil wrongdoing), and protecting individual rights secured by society. Frank Michelman, *The Supreme Court and Litigation Access Fees: The Right to Protect One's Rights—Part I*, 1973 DUKE L.J. 1153, 1172–77 (1973). The Supreme Court seems to have concluded, at least for the current era, that these interests do not constitutionally require states or the United States

to provide their impoverished residents with free legal assistance in civil cases. United States v. Kras, 409 U.S. 434 (1973); Ortwein v. Schwab, 410 U.S. 656 (1973). However, these considerations may persuade legislatures of the desirability of making such provisions. I am grateful to Professor David Luban for referring me to Professor Michelman's analysis.

82. NAT'L ASS'N FOR LAW PLACEMENT, *supra* note 44, at 30.

83. Mark Hansen, *supra* note 43, at 24.

84. NAT'L JURIST ON LINE, *supra* note 42.

85. Ibid.

86. SANDY BAUM & DIANE SAUNDERS, LIFE AFTER DEBT: RESULTS OF THE NATIONAL STUDENT LOAN SURVEY (monograph published by Nellie Mae) 42 (1998). In 1997, 22 percent of respondents (as opposed to 12 percent in 1991) believed that debt had delayed their having children. Ibid.

87. Debtors with doctoral and professional degrees constituted only 7 percent of the survey population; those with a college degree or less (and therefore presumably much less indebted) constituted 75 percent. *Id.* at 43.

88. *Id.* at 29.

89. SANDY BAUM, GRADUATE AND PROFESSIONAL BORROWING: ARE EARNINGS HIGH ENOUGH TO SUPPORT DEBT LEVELS? 15 (monograph published by Nellie Mae Foundation) (1999).

90. "[S]tudents often aren't aware of the full extent of that debt—and its impact on their lifestyles—until they start thinking about looking for their first jobs. 'For most students, the light dawns some time in their second year,' said Mary Birmingham, placement director at the University of Arizona." Crittenden, *supra* note 55, at 17.

91. Already, at least one major law student lender has tightened credit criteria for law student borrowers. Stabile, *supra* note 43, at 17.

92. Jeffrey E. Hanson, *Critical Challenges in Financing Graduate and Professional Degrees, in* ACCESS GROUP, SYMPOSIUM ON HIGHER EDUCATION FINANCING, CRITICAL CHALLENGES IN FINANCING GRADUATE AND PROFESSIONAL DEGREES 10 (1997). In 1996, thirty-six law schools had default rates exceeding 15 percent and faced restrictions on student borrowing. Mary Geraghty, *Deep in Debt, More Law-School Graduates Are Defaulting on Their Student Loans,* CHRON. HIGHER EDUC., Aug. 2, 1996, at A27.

93. Such inefficiencies may include, for example, entering students' lack of knowledge about cost and debt, and the possible tendency of some voters to subordinate their long-term desire to promote greater public service to their short-term interest in reducing taxes by paying fewer subsidies.

94. Another way to put the point is that, as every first-year economics student learns, even when markets are efficient, they may not produce "just" results because of an initial or continuing maldistribution of

wealth or income. The United States has a huge gap between the resources of its wealthy citizens and those of its poorest citizens. In the mid-1980s, the wealthiest ½ of 1 percent of the U.S. population was estimated to own 27 percent of the nation's resources, up from 14 percent in 1976. In 1988, families in the lowest quintile of the population (under $15,102 annual income) had 5 percent of the income, while the highest quintile had 44 percent, a gap that was increasing with time. KEVIN PHILLIPS, THE POLITICS OF RICH AND POOR 12–13, 241 (1991). By 1999, the lowest fifth was down to 4 percent of the after-tax income, while the highest fifth had more than 50 percent, and the richest 1 percent (those with household after-tax income in excess of $515,600) had as much after-tax income as all of the people in the bottom 38 percent. ISAAC SHAPIRO & ROBERT GREENSTEIN, THE WIDENING INCOME GULF (CENTER ON BUDGET AND POLICY PRIORITIES, 1999), http://www.cbpp.org/9-4—99tax-rep. htm. Wealth continued to be even more concentrated than income. By 1995, the concentration of wealth (39 percent of the nation's wealth) in the richest 1 percent of the population was greater than at any time since the Depression. Edward N. Wolff, *Top Heavy: A Study of the Increasing Inequality of Wealth in America*, A TWENTIETH CENTURY FUND REPORT (1995); Thomas N. Shapiro and Edward N. Wolff, *Assets and the Disadvantaged: The Benefits of Spreading Asset Ownership* (2001).

95. For a dated but still excellent account of the realm of public interest law, see *Comment, The New Public Interest Lawyers*, 79 YALE L.J. 1069 (1970). See also Jean Camper Cahn & Edgar Cahn, *Power to the People or the Profession? The Public Interest in Public Interest Law*, 79 YALE L.J. 1005 (1970).

96. The following discussion pertains to the legislation providing for subsidies for low-income graduates through income-contingent loan repayment option of the direct lending program, but it should be noted that the much older laws establishing student loan programs such as the Stafford loan programs also include subsidies. Stafford loans have three subsidies: (1) the government pays interest on up to $8,500 (subject to a very generous "need" test) of each year's loan while the student borrower is in school; (2) the next $10,000 is loaned at an advantageous low rate because the government guarantees the debt; and (3) loans are subject to a rate ceiling of 8.25 percent even if the market rate of interest is higher. Stafford loans arguably include two additional subsidies, although the point can be debated. The interest paid by Stafford borrowers while they are in school (or in a grace or deferment period) is 0.6 percent lower than the rate paid during ordinary repayment periods. 20 U.S.C. § 1077a(k)(2) (2000). This lower rate may reflect lower processing costs attributable to this period, but "there was in fact a budgetary basis for this statutory change [that] disproportionate[ly accrues] to borrowers, such as law students, who have the largest loans and stay in school for

the longest period of time." E-mail from a Department of Education official, to the author (Aug. 1, 2000) (on file with the author). Also, all Stafford loans are extended at the same interest rate, disproportionately benefitting students at schools where banks would otherwise charge higher rates because of higher default rates by alumni. When they make commercial loans because students have reached the ceiling on government-guaranteed loans, banks do in fact vary the rate by school. *See, e.g.*, the rates on Law Access loans offered by the Access Group, www.accessgroup.org. The 1993 legislation added further subsidies for high-debt, low-income borrowers, as described in the next chapter. In addition to these two features, which may or may not be subsidies for all Stafford borrowers, two other features lower rates for borrowers who obtain funds directly from the federal government rather than through FFELP. Direct borrowers receive an immediate interest rebate of 1.5 percent of the loan, though to keep it, they must make their first twelve payments on time. This rebate is the equivalent of about ¼ of 1 percent over the life of a ten-year loan. Second, students who consolidate their loans from FFELP into direct federal loans receive a new interest rate 0.8 of 1 percent lower than their current payment; again, they must make the first twelve payments on time to keep the lower rate. White House Press Release, *The Clinton-Gore Administration: Making College More Affordable and Accessible for America's Families*, http://www.pub.whitehouse.gov/urichres/I2R?urn:pdi://oma.eop.gov.us/2000/8/10/8.text.1 (Aug. 10, 2000, last visited Sept. 8, 2000). The federal government is also preparing to offer an additional subsidy in the form of loan repayment, up to $6,000 per year, to a small group of student borrowers, those who decide to work for the government itself. Kenneth J. Cooper, *U.S. May Repay Loans for College*, WASH. POST, Dec. 13, 2000, at A45.

# 2

# Congress to the Rescue

## THE 1993 LEGISLATION

In 1993, after a considerable legislative struggle, Congress created a new federal program that would compete with the banks offering FFELP loans. Through the new federal direct lending program, the U.S. Department of Education would offer its own loans to students. Direct loans would eliminate the "middleman" banking entities that earn substantial federal fees on FFELP loans while taking few risks, since the federal government guarantees the FFELP loans.

Ironically, the policy of making it easier for heavily indebted graduates to engage in public service was a major driving force behind the new law, although as yet there is little indication that this policy is being effectuated. As we shall see, even heavily indebted, socially conscious law graduates, the group that might be most likely to benefit from the novel "income-contingent repayment option" that Congress required for federal direct loans, do not know much about or want to use the plan.

The history of the law's enactment is told in Steven Waldman's book, *The Bill*,[1] and summarized for student borrowers in Anne Stockwell's popular handbook.[2] Three factors coalesced during the 1989–93 Bush administration to start direct lending on a path to Congressional enactment. First, the Credit Reform Act of 1990 changed the way that the government accounted for student loans, so that the expense of making good on expected FFELP defaults had to be counted as governmental expenditures in the year that loans were made. This law ended a practice under which FFELP loans seemed costless to the government, and it made any future direct loans seem at least as competitive as, and perhaps more profitable than, FFELP loans.[3] Second, Republican Representative Tom Petri, who over the years had become an expert on student loans and a critic of FFELP, began to advocate more vigorously within the Bush administration for the creation of a direct lending program. Among Petri's ideas was a concept originally advocated by the conservative economist Milton Friedman[4]: allowing the annual amount of a student loan repayment to depend on the student's income, treating the loan as the lender's investment in the student's future success, on which dividends should be returned if there is enough income to pay them.[5] However, Petri believed that income-contingent repayment could be managed only through direct lending, not through FFELP. He believed that the administration of a repayment program linked to income could be managed only by the Internal Revenue Service, to which all income was reported. Third, in the White House, Republican economist Charles Kolb devised the mechanics of a direct loan program under which "the [FFELP] banks would be eliminated [because] Uncle Sam could raise the same money more cheaply. . . . The . . . existing program would be replaced by a streamlined system that maximized efficiency and minimized cost."[6] In 1992, Congress even passed a law through which the federal government would create a federal direct loan demonstration project, in which students at a small number of schools would be able to obtain loans with income-contingent repayment.[7]

Just as the ideas of direct lending and income-contingent repayment were gaining currency in Washington, D.C., Bill Clinton was on the campaign trail advocating creation of a national public service program (which was eventually enacted and became AmeriCorps).[8] Late in the campaign, he coupled income-contingent repayments with the idea of national service, reasoning that students resisted public service in part because they incurred so much debt.[9] Clinton suggested that reducing loan repayments would "remove extra weight from the shoulders of someone who is inclined toward a public service career," and he thought that addressing this problem would particularly benefit graduate students.[10] He deeply believed that "people are not really free" if they can not take advantage of their God-given potential, and that by reducing debt, the government could enable young Americans to serve others.[11] At a White House meeting during the first month of his administration, Bill Clinton's advisors briefed him on the concept of direct federal lending. He responded by lecturing the advisors, saying that what was important to him was income-contingent repayment, not direct lending. "The direct loan is a good thing," President Clinton argued, "but that's not the core of my proposal. Everywhere we went [in the campaign], people responded to this [idea for facilitating public service]." Senators who would eventually become leaders in the effort for legislative approval of the program agreed with him.[12]

Originally, the president wanted a single bill to create a national service corps and an income-contingent repayment plan, but loan reform had to have its own bill because it had to go through a Congressional process quite different from the process of setting up a new agency.[13] The loan bill was introduced by Senator Edward Kennedy on May 5, 1993; the bill stated that one of its purposes was to "provide a variety of repayment plans, including income-contingent repayment . . . to borrowers so that . . . [their] obligations do not foreclose community service-oriented career choices."[14] In his introductory remarks, Senator Kennedy stated that income contingency would make it possible for students to pursue careers and to take lower paying jobs that "they prefer, including careers in public service and community service."[15] During its progress through Congress, the bill was the subject of heavy attacks from the banking industry, which was intent on preserving the FFELP,[16] but it picked up many supporters who were particularly attracted by the possibility that it could encourage greater public service.[17]

The public service aspect of income-contingent repayment was also highlighted at the hearings of the Senate Committee on Labor and Human Resources. Senator Kennedy called it a "companion feature" of direct lending and said that "no college student should be forced to become a lawyer or investment banker who would rather be a teacher."[18] Senator Claiborne Pell said that the repayment plan "could also help students to enter public service occupations which often, and unfortunately, do not carry high salaries."[19] Deputy Secretary of Education Madeleine Kunin noted that the option "will allow students to enter lower paying community service jobs."[20] R. Marshall Witten, speaking for the National Commission on Responsibilities for Financing Postsecondary Education, strongly endorsed income-contingent repayment because it would offer borrowers "loan forgiveness for public and community service."[21] Claire Roemer, testifying for the National Association of Student Financial Aid Administrators, opposed new direct lending legislation but recognized the value of income-contingent repayment because it would enable borrowers to "consider lower-paying community service jobs."[22]

The Senate Committee recommended passage of the bill, noting that "income-contingent repayment will allow students to take lower paying community and public service jobs without the fear of being overburdened with loan debt. . . . [The option is] intended to accommodate borrowers whose income after graduation . . . is low, and thus would be attractive to borrowers who plan to enter lower-paying community service jobs."[23]

Similarly, the report of the House Committee on Education and Labor, incorporated in the report of the House Budget Committee, stated that one of the purposes of the legislation was to provide "an income-contingent repayment plan . . . so that borrowers['] . . . obligations do not foreclose community service-oriented career choices for them."[24] The report added that "any student wanting to take a lower-paying job that services his or her community would be encouraged to do so through flexible and affordable repayment terms for education loans."[25] The income-contingent option would "permit students to pursue public service either for a few years after completing their education or as a career since their loan burden need never be disproportionate to their income."[26]

A conference committee reconciled the Senate[27] and House[28] versions of the bill.[29] The real battle between the versions was fought over whether direct lending would entirely supplant FFELP. By contrast, the details of direct lending, such as income-contingent repayment, were uncontroversial.[30] As approved by the conference committee and soon thereafter by both houses of Congress, the legislation created the federal direct lending program, leaving many of the details to be established by regulation. It required the secretary of education to offer borrowers four repayment plans: standard ten-year repayment; "extended" repayment over a longer period of time; "graduated" repayment, in which the amount to be repaid would increase as the loan aged; and income-contingent repayment. The income-contingent provision provided that annual repayment amounts would be "based on the income of the borrower," giving the secretary wide latitude to establish repayment schedules. It also specified that the period of repayment was "not to exceed 25 years," implicitly authorizing the secretary to cancel or forgive outstanding balances at the end of that period, since Congress did not authorize continuing collection of the debt after twenty-five years.[31]

Imposing some limit after which student loans would not be collected was necessary, because without it the amount due on a student loan paid through an income-contingent plan could forever rise, as payments deferred by the income-related cap continued to be added to the remaining principal. Without some time limit, the former student could pay for his or her entire life, and the student's estate could be liable after that. However, Congress did not give much thought to the length of time after which debts would be forgiven. The bill that the Department of Education had drafted for Congressional consideration did not specify this or any other detail, because in early 1993 "the department [as opposed to the president] still didn't fully buy into the importance of flexible repayment; it viewed direct lending as a major reform, and [income-contingent] repayment as a minor convenience."[32] The House bill did not specify a period. On this issue, staff members to two Republican senators made an important contribution to the legislation. When the Senate bill was being edited, aides to Senators Nancy Kassebaum and James Jeffords "suggested that no student should have to pay off a loan for more than twenty years. [Senator Paul Simon's aide] and the other staffers agreed. Although the discussion took about ten minutes . . . these Senate Republican staffers had made the reform dramatically more progressive, establishing a much stronger incentive for public service than Clinton's own Department of Education."[33] The conference committee resolved the difference between the House and Senate provisions on income-contingent repayment with the "not to exceed 25 years" formula. To ensure that *any* borrower could use income-contingent repayment, even if the borrower had originally borrowed through FFELP rather than through a federal direct loan, Congress also provided that the government had to offer a consolidation loan, repayable through the income-contingent plan, to any FFELP borrower.[34]

The debate on final passage added no further relevant legislative history. Senator Simon noted simply that "at the heart of the program is President Clinton's promise to allow students to pay off their loans as a percentage of income, so that no one is prevented from serving the country as a teacher, rural health worker, or other valuable yet lower paying profession."[35]

## THE INCOME-CONTINGENT REPAYMENT FORMULA

Shortly after Congress passed the law, the Department of Education began a process of fleshing out its details through regulations. The current version of the regulations, summarized here, is set forward in Appendix A of this volume. These regulations have been amended from time to time, but they have remained substantially similar, and they offer two new subsidies that are not available to Stafford loan borrowers who elect other repayment methods. A borrower may consolidate all government-guaranteed loans (even a single loan) into a federal direct loan and may elect to pay under the income-contingent repayment option.[36] As in the case of all consolidated federal loans, the interest rate is fixed, and it is determined on the date of consolidation by computing the weighted average of the underlying loans. (Until consolidation, the rate on those underlying loans is variable and is the ninety-one-day Treasury bill rate for the last auction during the preceding May, plus 1.7 percent or 2.3 percent, subject to the statutory cap of 8.25 percent).[37] The borrower repays the debt over a twenty-five-year period, unless it is paid off earlier than that,[38] but in each and every year, the amount payable is limited to a specified part of the borrower's income for the previous year. The borrower is required to pay only the amount produced by whichever of two formulas produces the lower number.[39] One of the two formulas, "the discretionary income method,"[40] produces most of the calculations that are important for high-debt, low-income law graduates.[41]

This method defines the graduate's discretionary income as the borrower's adjusted gross income,[42] minus the federal poverty level for a family of the borrower's family size. The borrower must repay only 20 percent of his or her discretionary income.[43] The federal poverty level is adjusted annually; in 2000, it was $8,350 for a single person and $11,250 for a couple.[44] Thus, for an individual with adjusted gross income of $28,350,[45] the repayment obligation would be 20 percent of $20,000, or $4,000 per year ($333 per month). For a person with $55,000 of consolidated debt, the $333 per month repayment obligation is much lower than the "standard" repayment of $674. Of course, if the borrower's income rises, the annual repayment will rise, but it will never be more than 20 percent of the discretionary income.[46]

The $333 monthly payment in this example is also lower than the $434 that would be owed under a simple twenty-five-year amortization of the $55,000. Under income-contingent repayment, the $101 that is not paid each month because of the income-related cap is added to the outstanding principal balance. However, once the principal balance increases to an amount that is 10 percent higher than the borrower's original balance, the government stops adding the unpaid interest to the balance.[47] Once the principal has reached this 110 percent level, the interest that is unpaid as a result of the income-related cap is merely accumulated in a dummy account and is not again added to the principal. Even after the borrower later works the principal balance down to less than 110 percent of the original principal, new unpaid interest is placed only in this new dummy account. The borrower owes the federal government the balance in the dummy account, as well as the balance in the regular account, but the dummy account funds are not subject to compounding. If and when the borrower is able to pay more than the amount due for the current month within the limits of his or her monthly income-contingent cap, he or she will begin to work down the balance in the dummy account as well.[48] The noncompounding of unpaid interest after the borrower first increases the principal balance by 10 percent is the first of two additional subsidies[49] provided to high-debt, low-income borrowers who use the income-contingent plan.

Payments that must be remitted because they are within the income-contingent repayment formula (i.e., less than 20 percent of the difference between the borrower's adjusted gross income and the poverty level) must be paid monthly.[50] Because the repayment period is so long, and interest continues to accrue even though it may not be added to the principal, the amount of money that will eventually have to be paid is much larger, even taking the subsidy into account, than under standard repayment.

The borrower may switch out of income-contingent repayment, electing standard repayment or a different repayment plan, at any time.[51] If the borrower remains in the income-contingent plan and experiences good income increases, the principal balance might be paid off in less than twenty-five years. However, if the borrower is not so fortunate as to pay off the loan within that time, the federal government will forgive the entire remaining balance, including the principal and accrued interest, at the end of the twenty-fifth year.[52] This is the second additional subsidy built into the income-contingent repayment option, potentially offering significant benefits to graduates who plan entire careers in low-paying jobs.

Married couples who borrow may pool their individual debts for purposes of income-contingent repayment.[53] However, married couples who do not elect to pool their debts, and even those who file separate tax returns, are deemed to pool their income for purposes of determining the monthly repayment obligation.[54] Thus the plan includes a significant "marriage penalty" for married, two-income, one-debt couples (compared to the repayment obligations of similar couples who do not marry). More will be said about this in chapters 5 and 7.

Because the income-contingent repayment option offers two subsidies for low-income borrowers, including a potentially very large subsidy after twenty-five years, one might think that law students contemplating low-paying public interest careers would be keenly aware of and interested in this repayment method, which was enacted with people like them in mind. However, nothing could be further from the truth.

## NOTES

1. STEVEN WALDMAN, THE BILL (1995).

2. ANNE STOCKWELL, THE GUERRILLA GUIDE TO MASTERING STUDENT LOAN DEBT (1997).

3. STOCKWELL, *supra* note 2, at 86–87.

4. Milton Friedman, *The Role of Government in Education, in* CAPITALISM AND FREEDOM 100–07 (1962).

5. STOCKWELL, *supra* note 2, at 84–87. In his presidential campaign in 1988, Massachusetts Governor Michael Dukakis had also advocated creation of a federal income-contingent loan repayment plan. Barbara Vobejda, *Dukakis Student Loan Plan Gets Mixed Reviews in Theory, Practice,* WASH. POST, Sept. 9, 1988, at A23.

6. CHARLES KOLB, WHITE HOUSE DAZE: THE UNMAKING OF DOMESTIC POLICY IN THE BUSH YEARS 147–48 (1998).

7. Higher Education Amendments of 1992, Pub. L. No. 102–325, § 416, 106 Stat. 529 (1992).

8. WALDMAN, *supra* note 1, at 9–14, 239.

9. *Id.* at 6.

10. *Id.* at 31.

11. *Id.* at 31–32.

12. In 1992, Senator Paul Simon had said that income-contingency "helps to ensure that debt does not drive students into particular professions just so that they'll be able to pay off their loans." *Income-contingent Student Loans*, 138 CONG. REC. S4675–76 (daily ed., Apr. 1, 1992). When the 103d Congress opened, Senator David Durenberger urged the president's nominee for secretary of education to make an income-contingent loan program a high priority. David Durenberger, *Statement on the Nomination of Richard W. Riley*, 139 CONG. REC. S93 (daily ed., Jan. 21, 1993).

13. The direct lending bill had to go into the budget reconciliation bill because it saved money that could be used to offset other budget expenditures. The national service bill could not go into the reconciliation bill because, under Senate rules, new programs could not be created through a budget reconciliation bill. WALDMAN, *supra* note 1, at 275.

14. Student Loan Reform of 1993, S. 920, 103d Cong., 139 CONG. REC. S5646–47 (daily ed., May 6, 1993).

15. 139 CONG. REC. S5585 (daily ed., May 6, 1993).

16. WALDMAN, *supra* note 1, at 131, 159.

17. *See, e.g.*, 139 CONG. REC. S5637 (daily ed. May 6, 1993) (remarks of Sen. Christopher Dodd) (income contingency will "allow many of today's graduates to consider lower-paying, community-oriented jobs, or career paths that will provide the kind of personal satisfaction that so many seek without necessarily providing the kind of financial success of other more lucrative careers"); 139 CONG. REC. S5641 (daily ed., May 6, 1993) (remarks of Sen. James Jeffords) ("it is naive of us to think that we can attract energetic and bright individuals into community and social service when they have living expenses and education costs to think about."); and 139 CONG. REC. S5641–42 (daily ed., May 6, 1993) (remarks of Sen. Paul Wellstone) ("quite often, if you have a huge loan . . . you are not going to have an opportunity to do a lot of the kind of work that needs to be done in this country but could not pay much by way of wages").

18. *Student Loan Reform: Hearing on S. 920 before the Senate Committee on Labor and Human Resources*, 103d Cong., 1st Sess., 2 (May 26, 1993).

19. *Id.* at 5.

20. *Id.* at 34.

21. *Id.* at 76.

22. *Id.* at 6.

23. STAFF OF SENATE COMM. ON THE BUDGET, 103D CONG., RECONCIL-IATION SUBMISSIONS OF THE INSTRUCTED COMMITTEES PURSUANT TO THE CONCURRENT RESOLUTION ON THE BUDGET (H. CON. RES. 64) 447 (Comm. Print 1993) (reprinting submission of Senate Committee on Labor and Human Resources of report language to accompany Title XII of the Budget Reconciliation Act).

24. HOUSE COMM. ON THE BUDGET, Report 103–111, at 112, *reprinted in* 1993 U.S.C.C.A.N. 378, 480 (1993).

25. *Id.* at 106, 1993 U.S.C.C.A.N. at 474.

26. *Id.* at 107, 1993 U.S.C.C.A.N. at 475.

27. H.R. 2264, 103d Cong., as passed by the Senate, June 25, 1993.

28. H.R. 2264, 103d Cong. (May 27, 1993).

29. Conference Report on Omnibus Budget Reconciliation, 139 CONG. REC. H6272 (daily ed. Aug. 5, 1993).

30. The House bill would have replaced FFELP with direct federal lending immediately. The Senate bill would have allowed 50 percent of lending to be direct lending. The compromise that emerged allowed a phase-in of direct lending, leading to a federal extension of more than 60 percent of student loans by the fifth year of the five-year legislative authorization. See WALDMAN, *supra* note 1, at 204, 222, 230, 235.

31. Omnibus Budget Reconciliation Act of 1993, Pub. L. No. 103–66, § 455, 107 Stat. 312 (1993).

32. WALDMAN, *supra* note 1, at 157.

33. *Id.* 157–58.

34. Congress did this by providing that a federal consolidation loan should be offered to any borrower who "is unable to obtain a consolidation loan with income-sensitive repayment terms acceptable to the borrower from such a lender." H.R. 2264, § 4046, 103d Cong. (1993). Since banks do not offer loan cancellation after twenty-five years, any borrower may obtain federal consolidation by regarding a bank loan without a forgiveness clause as unacceptable. The Department of Education made a decision not to require consolidating borrowers to document their inability to obtain a loan with acceptable terms from a private source. U.S. Department of Education, William D. Ford Federal Direct Loan Program; Final Rule, 59 Fed. Reg. 61,683 (Dec. 1, 1994). The legislation also provided that federal consolidation loans "shall, as requested by the borrower, be repaid either pursuant to income-contingent repayment . . . or pursuant to any other repayment provision" of the new law, thus specifying that consolidated FFELP loans, as well as loans that began as federal direct loans, were eligible for repayment through the income-contingent option. H.R. 2264, § 4046, 103d Cong. (1993).

35. 139 CONG. REC. S10680–81, 10729 (daily ed. Aug. 6, 1993).

36. 34 C.F.R. § 685.215 (1993).

37. 20 U.S.C. § 1077a(k)(4) (2000)); 34 C.F.R. §§ 685.215(g); 685.202(a)(1)(ii) (1993). Students who consolidate quickly in the months after graduation are able to lock in the lower rate (1.7 percent above the last auction rate) for the life of the consolidated loan. U.S. Department of Education, "Dear Colleague" letter, GEN-99–77, June 18, 1999, at http://ifap.ed.gov/dev_csb/new/drcollg.nsf/e45795ae60c28d8685266f1005ba6ad/09cb025ddcdc3b838525679a00452b69?OpenDocument.

38. The regulations provide that the "maximum" period for income-contingent repayment is twenty-five years, implying that a borrower might elect a shorter period, or that the Secretary of Education could agree to a shorter one. 34 C.F.R. § 685.209(c)(4)(I) (2000). At present, only a twenty-five-year loan is eligible for forgiveness of the balance remaining at the end of the repayment period. § 685.209(c)(4) (iv).

39. 34 C.F.R. § 209(a)(2) (2000).

40. 34 C.F.R. § 685.209(a)(2)(ii) (2000).

41. The alternative formula caps annual repayment at the amount the borrower would repay annually through twelve-year amortization, multiplied by an "income percentage factor" published annually in a Federal Register table that links this factor to the level of the borrower's income. 34 C.F.R. § 685.209(a)(2)(I) (2000). This alternative formula is lower than the formula discussed in the text only for certain borrowers with relatively low debts. It has some impact on high-debt, low-income borrowers, however, because toward the end of their periods of repayment, their balances may become low enough that the alternative formula produces a lower repayment amount. The income-contingent repayment calculator described in this book computes monthly, annual, and total payments based on whatever formula produces lower monthly payments.

42. Adjusted gross income is defined in federal tax law. For most practical purposes, it is the same as gross (pretax) income. However, payments of a portion of student loan interest, moving expenses, and alimony payments, as well as a few less frequently encountered expenditures, are deducted from gross income before arriving at adjusted gross income. See INTERNAL REVENUE SERVICE, YOUR FEDERAL INCOME TAX FOR INDIVIDUALS (Pub. 17) 117 (2000).

43. The borrower must consent to allow the Internal Revenue Service to disclose the borrower's adjusted gross income to the Department of Education. 34 C.F.R § 209(c)(7) (2000).

44. 2000 HHS Poverty Guidelines, http://aspe.hhs.gov/poverty/00poverty.htm (last visited June 29, 2000). $2,900 is added for each dependent, and the numbers are higher in Alaska and Hawaii. Ibid.

45. This number was chosen to make the example simple, but it is not an impossibly low salary for a person beginning a public interest job. In

2000, 35 percent of starting salaries in legal services offices were $29,000 or less. *See* Table 5.4.

46. Because "discretionary income" is defined by the formula and is not the same as after-tax income, payments as a percentage of after-tax income can be slightly higher than 20 percent. However, as the tables in this book show, payment obligations higher than 20 percent are rare and occur mainly for borrowers with very high incomes, not for high-debt, low-income taxpayers. High-income taxpayers could lower their payments by electing different income repayment plans.

47. 34 C.F.R. § 685.209(c)(5) (2000).

48. This unpaid interest will be added to principal only if the borrower reconsolidates the debt (or in the case of a loan that was a direct federal loan from the beginning, consolidates it) or defaults. Neither the combination of two debtors' income-contingent debts, as a result of marriage, nor election of a different repayment schedule is considered a consolidation. However, if the borrower changes repayment plans, the accrued interest in the dummy account must be scheduled for payment. Thus, if the borrower moves out of income-contingent repayment and elects ten-year amortization of the remaining debt, he or she must pay $\frac{1}{120}$ of the balance in the dummy account each month, but the part of the dummy account that is not paid during the first month remains in a special account and still is not capitalized, so it does not accumulate additional interest. Similarly, if a borrower wins the lottery and decides to prepay the debt all at once, the accumulated additional interest must be paid at that time. This information was based on a telephone interview on July 5, 2000, with a Department of Education official who was familiar with the Department's algorithm for computing the balance due on income-contingent loans but did not want to be identified by name.

49. See chapter 1, note 96, for a description of the three subsidies generally available to Stafford borrowers.

50. These payments would be those that would be due under a twenty-five-year extended repayment plan, subject to the. income-contingent cap. Within the limit established by the cap, the borrower first pays the interest and principal that would be due under the twenty-five-year extended repayment formula, and, if within that limit, any money can be paid from the dummy account created because the borrower's principal had at some point climbed by 10 percent, that money is due as well.

51. The regulations purport to permit switching from income-contingent to standard repayment only during the first ten years of income-contingent repayment. 34 C.F.R. § 685.210(a)(2)(I) (2000). However, a borrower "may prepay all or part of a loan at any time without penalty." 34 C.F.R. § 685.211(a)(2) (2000). Thus, a borrower who

wants to elect ten-year repayment after paying under income-contingency for, say, eleven years, could use any Web-based ten-year repayment calculator to compute the monthly payments for the remaining principal balance paid over ten years (rather than the remaining fourteen years), and then make those payments for ten years until the debt was fully repaid. Similarly, a borrower could devise a graduated repayment plan.

52. 34 C.F.R. § 685.209(c)(4)(iv) (2000).
53. 34 C.F.R. § 685.209(b)(2) (2000).
54. 34 C.F.R. § 685.209(b)(1) (2000).

# 3

# The Student Response

During the spring of 1999, I surveyed law students at Georgetown University and Catholic University to ascertain what they knew about the income-continent repayment option, and (whether or not they knew about it before my survey explained it to them) their views about using it to pay off their own debts. Both schools are located in Washington, D.C. Both are private schools affiliated with the Catholic Church. Both have high tuition in an area of the country with a relatively high cost of living. The two schools differ, however, in that Georgetown University has a Loan Repayment Assistance Program,[1] through which it repays some of the debt of low-income graduates who work in public interest jobs, whereas Catholic University does not.[2]

Georgetown University Law Center is one of the nation's largest law schools. In 1998–99, 1,553 students were enrolled. The Law Center charged $24,530 annual tuition, and it estimated living expenses at $14,720. Average debt at graduation was $82,600 (including an estimated $9,500 of undergraduate debt). Sixty-six percent of its most recent graduates were employed in law firms, 5 percent in business, 14 percent in government (other than as judicial clerks), 8 percent as clerks, and 3 percent in public interest law.

At the time of the survey, Catholic University Law School had 902 students. Its tuition was $23,898, and living expenses were estimated at $13,390. Average debt was $78,500 (including the average college debt). Forty-seven percent of its recent graduates worked in law firms, 19 percent in business, 18 percent in government, 10 percent in clerkships, and 3 percent in public interest law.[3]

At each school, the author's surveys and a follow-up reminder were placed in each student's individual mailbox, and responses were returned to a central location.[4] The questionnaires did not include space for the respondent's name or other identifying information, and they were returned anonymously to a central location. At Georgetown, 390 students (25 percent) responded; at Catholic, 131 students (14 percent).

Table 3.1 summarizes certain relevant characteristics of the students who responded. It recapitulates their class in law school; membership in Georgetown's Equal Justice Foundation (EJF) or Catholic's Students for Public Interest Law (SPIL), which promote interest in public interest law;[5] and intention to go into a government or public interest job immediately after graduation. For those students (about two-thirds of all respondents) who indicated a desire (if debt were not a factor) to spend at least one-third of their careers doing public service, the table also reports average anticipated government-guaranteed debt (including college debt); average anticipated total debt; and the percentage of respondents whose anticipated total debt (rounded to the nearest $10,000) was, in the categorization I used for purposes of analyzing survey responses, "low" (zero through $60,000), high ($70,000 through $90,000), or very high ($100,000 or more).

A few aspects of Table 3.1 are worth noting. First, I was somewhat concerned that my sample would be unrepresentative because only the students who cared most about public interest law would respond to the questionnaire, but as measured by affiliation with the public interest student organization, at neither school was the group of respondents top-heavy with students who were members of the relevant core group. Second, among those asked to report debt at both schools, the average anticipated government-guaranteed debt exceeded three times the annual Stafford ceiling on law school loans, reflecting students' borrowing up to the limit of Stafford loans, accruing some interest on them, and also owing government-guaranteed loans from college. Finally, the total anticipated debt levels were very high. Nearly half of the students who want to do substantial amounts of public service work during their careers expect to graduate owing at least $100,000.[6] Nine percent of each survey's students expect to graduate owing at least $130,000.

I first sought to ascertain the respondents' career choices, because I was primarily interested in learning about loan repayment by students planning careers in public interest law. I defined "public interest" work as full-time legal work for a nonprofit organization or government agency, and I reminded respondents that these organizations generally had starting salaries in the range of $25,000 to $37,000. I asked, "If the burden of your student loans were *not* a consideration, what part of your

**Table 3.1**
**Characteristics of the Respondents**

| Characteristic | Students from | |
|---|---|---|
| | Georgetown (N=390) | Catholic (N=131) |
| Year of Law School | 1: 29%<br>2: 32%<br>3: 35%<br>4: 4% [a] | 1: 46%<br>2: 32%<br>3: 22% |
| Membership in EJF or SPIL | 22% | 19% |
| Intending to Take a Public Interest Job Immediately after Graduation (Or after a Post-Graduation Clerkship) [b] | 23% | 43% |
| Amount of Government-Guaranteed Debt of Public Interest-Oriented Students (Average) [c] | $63,095 | $58,064 |
| Total Debt of Such Students (Average) [d] | $95,495 | $94,615 |
| % Whose Debt Will Fall into Each Range | Low: 19%<br>High: 38%<br>Very High: 43% | Low: 25%<br>High: 26%<br>Very High: 49% |

[a] Includes evening students and students in a four-year joint degree program.

[b] The numbers reported in this row pertain to all respondents, not only those who want to spend at least one-third of their careers doing public service work. They are higher (and in the case of Catholic, substantially higher) than the actual numbers reported for government and public interest employment to the American Bar Association. However, the ABA statistics report judicial clerkships as a separate category of employment, and some of the clerks go on to government or public interest jobs. Also, students while in school may have intentions to do public interest work in the short term that are not ultimately fulfilled. Finally, the sample of students responding to this survey (particularly at Catholic) may have overrepresented students who planned to do public interest work immediately after graduation or a clerkship. If so, this is not a significant problem for the survey research, because the principal goal of the survey was to learn about the knowledge and attitudes of these very students (as opposed to all students) regarding the income-contingent loan repayment program, and most of the questions were directed only to that subgroup.

[c] Data only for respondents who reported a desire, were it not for debt, to spend at least one-third of their careers in public interest work. Those desiring to spend less than this percentage were not asked about debt.

[d] Data only for respondents who reported a desire, were it not for debt, to spend at least one-third of their careers in public interest work. Those desiring to spend less than this percentage were not asked about debt. The comparison of these numbers with those reported by schools to U.S. News and World Report suggests that the debts of these respondents may have been somewhat higher than average, perhaps because these respondents are the ones most interested in public service, and they may have earned less money than others in summer jobs during law school. Two other possible factors could account for the differences. First, the U.S. News and World Report data for debt reported on the class that graduated in 1998. Some of the students in my 1999 survey would not graduate until 2001, and expenses (and debts) were continuing to rise. Second, students with the highest debts may have been underrepresented in the responses to schools that were reported to the media, rather than overrepresented in my survey.

**Table 3.2**
**Students' Ideal of Portion of Career Spent on Public Interest Work**

| Fraction of Career | Students from | |
|---|---|---|
| | Georgetown (N=387) | Catholic (N=131) |
| Less than ⅓ | 33% | 24% |
| ⅓ to ⅔ | 33% | 38% |
| More than ⅔ | 34% | 37% |

*Note*: The responses did not vary substantially by class in law school. At Georgetown, for example, the proportion who wanted to spend more than two-thirds of their careers doing public service work fell only slightly from 39% of the first-year respondents to 32% of the third-year respondents.

legal career would you like to spend doing full-time public interest work?" The results are displayed in Table 3.2.

As might be expected, interest in lifelong public interest work (more than two-thirds) was higher among EJF members (41 percent) and SPIL members (72 percent) than among respondents as a whole, but there was also a correlation between the size of the anticipated debt and expected first post–law school employment. Table 3.3 shows a significant fall-off, as debt rises, in the expectation of doing public service work in the short term.

The students who did not want to do public interest work, regardless of debt, were not my principal focus, but I did want to contribute marginally to the literature on nondebt influences on law students' decisions not to pursue public interest careers.[7] I therefore asked one question exclusively to respondents who indicated a desire, regardless of debt level, to spend less than one-third of their careers on public interest work: What accounted for their choice? Were they motivated primarily by a desire for the greater remuneration offered by the private sector or by noneconomic factors (e.g., interest in business, or greater anticipated intellectual stimulation in a law firm)? Table 3.4 summarizes the quite similar responses of students at the two schools, nearly half of whom reported that they were primarily affected by the huge income differential (even before the large salary jump of 2000) between the private and public sectors. As one student commented, "these [public interest] salaries are simply too low to expect attorneys to want these jobs. . . . Anyone who had a career before [attending] law school . . . probably made the same or more money before starting . . . legal education. . . . [so] the price you are asked to pay is simply too high compared to private sector employment."[8]

The approximately two-thirds of the respondents who expressed a de-

**Table 3.3**
**Percentage of Students Expecting to Take Public Interest Jobs Immediately after Graduation or Clerkship, by Expected Debt**

| Amount of Debt | Students from | |
|---|---|---|
| | Georgetown | Catholic |
| Low ($60,000 or Less) | 60% (25 out of 42) | 72% (16 out of 22) |
| High ($70,000-$90,000) | 25% (21 out of 83) | 72% (16 out of 22) |
| Very High ($100,000 or More) | 30% (30 out of 100) | 36% (16 out of 45) |

*Note*: Data reported only for respondents who reported a desire, were it not for debt, to spend at least one-third of their careers in public interest work.

**Table 3.4**
**Primary Reason for Greater Interest in Private Sector Work**

| Stated Reason | Students from | |
|---|---|---|
| | Georgetown (N=128) | Catholic (N=32) |
| Need or Expect More Money than Public Interest Jobs Pay | 43% | 41% |
| Non-financial Reasons | 51% | 53% |
| Other | 6% | 6% |

sire, but for debt, to spend at least one-third of their careers on public interest work were asked many other questions. (All of the remaining tables report responses only from those students who, if debt considerations were disregarded, wanted to spend at least one-third of their careers doing public interest work). First, I eliminated the counter-factual hypothetical so that I could focus on the impact of debt. I asked: "Taking the reality of student loans, along with other financial realities and all other concerns into account, do you actually expect to spend at least one-third of your legal career dong full-time public interest work?" Table 3.5 shows that when financial realities are factored in, public service falls off by about 50 percent, although the drop-off rate is less for EJF and SPIL members. The gap between aspirations and expectations is also considerably smaller among those with the lowest debt than among those with the highest debt, providing some evidence challenging the findings of those who have suggested that "contrary to commonly held beliefs, law school debt does not have a significant effect on attorneys' first job choice" and that the more significant influences on public interest career choice are race, preexisting career plans, law school grades and relative wages in various sectors of the profession."[9]

**Table 3.5**
**Among Students Wishing to Spend at Least One-Third of Career in Public Service, Percentage Who Expect to Do So**

| Category of Respondents | Students from | |
|---|---|---|
| | Georgetown | Catholic |
| All | 48% (124 of 261) | 47% (45 of 96) |
| Members of EJF or SPIL | 59% (43 of 73) | 68% (17 of 25) |
| Anticipating Low Debt | 68% (13 of 19) | 73% (8 of 11) |
| Anticipating High Debt | 42% (32 of 76) | 61% (14 of 23) |
| Anticipating Very High Debt | 48% (79 of 166) | 37% (23 of 62) |

The half of the respondents who desired to work as public interest lawyers but did not expect to do so were asked why they lacked that expectation. Specifically, I asked them to identify the factors accounting for at least 25 percent of their expectation not to do the public service work that they wanted to do. The choices were as follows:

- "I can't afford to take a public interest salary and still repay my student loans." (coded in Table 3.6 as "debt")
- "Even aside from the burden of student loan repayments, I want the higher pay or other tangible or intangible benefits that I think I could get in the private sector." (coded as "benefits")
- "I can't get or don't expect to be able to get a public interest job that would interest me." (coded as "qualifications")
- Other

Table 3.6 shows the spread of reasons, which exceed 100 percent because students could give more than one reason.

This result tends to confirm that debt is by far the most important factor causing law students to abandon public service aspirations. Of course, the data is self-reported, and although students responding to an anonymous questionnaire could gain no benefit by reporting debt rather than salary differentials as the most frequent reason for changing their career plans, they might be deceiving themselves because they feel that wanting more money (rather than rapid debt retirement) is shameful. However, it provides one additional evidentiary support for President Clinton's view that accumulated debt significantly interferes with public service choices.[10]

Before turning to questions about income-contingent repayment, I

**Table 3.6**
**Significant Reasons for Foregoing Public Interest Work**

| Stated Reason | Students from | |
|---|---|---|
| | Georgetown (N=137) | Catholic (N=51) |
| Debt | 90% | 92% |
| Benefits | 53% | 49% |
| Qualifications | 6% | 4% |
| Other | 10% | 16% |

asked students who desired to spend at least one-third of their careers in public interest law one additional question, but I asked a different question at each school because only Georgetown has a school-financed loan repayment assistance program (LRAP) for those who take public interest jobs. Georgetown has two such programs. LRAP-I is an entitlement program that can pay off all government-guaranteed debts within a few years for students earning less than a specified ceiling in a "nonprofit entity which has as one of its primary purposes the rendering of legal services to or on behalf of persons or organizations which could not otherwise obtain like services."[11] LRAP-II covers students who work at low pay for a government, but it is not an entitlement program; students share, pro-rata, in an annual appropriation.[12] At Georgetown, to measure knowledge of a loan repayment plan that was extremely close to home, I asked whether the students were planning to use this program. Nineteen percent of the students in question planned to apply for at least one of the two LRAPs. Thus, 81 percent of students interested in significant public interest law work did not plan to use their own law school's repayment plan. This 81 percent (199 students) who responded negatively were asked their reasons, and Table 3.7 explains them.

I asked the Catholic University students a different but related question: "Which of these statements best reflects the planning that you have done for paying back your student loans?" The choices were as follows:

- "When I graduate, I will not have incurred substantial student debt."
- "Before starting law school, I computed the amount of debt that I would graduate with and planned how I would repay it and still have the kind of career I want to have."
- "While in law school, I have figured out a good way to repay my loans and still have the kind of career I want to have."
- "I have not yet figured out a good way to repay my loans and still have the kind of career I want to have."

**Table 3.7**
**Reasons Georgetown Students Gave for Not Using LRAP Despite Wanting to Do Public Interest Work (N = 199)**

| Reason[a] | No. (%) Students |
|---|---|
| I Don't Know about Those Programs | 90 (45%) |
| The Work I Want to Do Wouldn't Qualify | 75 (38%) |
| The Programs Wouldn't Provide Enough Money Toward Meeting My Loan Repayment Needs | 47 (24%) |
| I Want to Earn a High Salary and Pay Off My Student Debt Before Considering Public Interest Work | 115 (58%) |
| Other | 22 (11%) |

[a]Respondents could give more than one reason.

**Table 3.8**
**Methods of Financial Planning by Catholic University Law Students Wanting Careers Involving Substantial Public Interest Work (N = 98)**

| Method of Planning | % Respondents |
|---|---|
| Analyzed Debt and Made Plan Before Starting School | 13% |
| Analyzed Debt and Made Plan During School | 12% |
| Haven't Yet Figured out a Plan | 68% |
| Will Incur No Substantial Debt | 6% |

Table 3.8 shows that the vast majority had not yet found a way to reconcile their debts with their career aspirations.

Turning to the income-contingent repayment option, I first gave a two-sentence description of the federal program without providing any details about its rules, and I asked respondents at both schools whether they had heard of it before receiving the questionnaire.[13] Table 3.9 shows that only 9 percent of the respondents had known about the plan even generally, and only an additional 24 percent to 30 percent had ever heard mention of it. At each school, more than 60 percent of these respondents—the target group for a plan to help those with the largest debts and lowest incomes—had never heard of the income-contingent repayment option.

The low awareness could have been accounted for, in part, by students attending to debt repayment only in their third year of school, when debt repayment loomed, but the survey showed no significantly increasing awareness as the date for repayment neared.[14] Table 3.10 shows the

**Table 3.9**
**Knowledge of the Income-Contingent Repayment Option**

| Response When Asked of Knowledge of Program | Students from | |
|---|---|---|
| | Georgetown (N=255) | Catholic (N=98) |
| No, Never Heard of it | 62% | 67% |
| Yes, but Only Vaguely and Didn't Know of its Provisions Even in General Terms | 30% | 24% |
| Yes, and Knew of Provisions at Least Generally | 9% | 9% |

**Table 3.10**
**Percentage of Respondents Unaware of the Option by Year of Law School**

| Year of Law School | Students from | |
|---|---|---|
| | Georgetown | Catholic |
| First | 60% | 67% |
| Second | 61% | 77% |
| Third | 64% | 47% |

percentage of respondents who were unaware of the option, by year of law school.

The degree of unawareness may, however, be somewhat related to the amount of debt, with the least-indebted students least aware of the option, as shown by Table 3.11.

About a third of students who expected at least $100,000 of debt had heard of the option. However, the percentage of these high-debt students who knew at least generally about its terms was only 8 percent at Georgetown and 9 percent at Catholic, no better than the percentage among all respondents at these schools.

The minority of students who had at least heard of the option were asked how they had heard of it and were allowed to respond with as many sources as were applicable. Table 3.12 shows that most of the information about the option had been received through word of mouth rather than from the government (either through printed literature or its website) or from other, more channeled, sources of information.[15]

The third of respondents who had heard of the program were asked whether they were planning to consolidate their loans and repay them through this plan.[16] Table 3.13 shows that less than a quarter of this third of respondents was planning to use it, and that a majority didn't know enough about it to make such a plan.

The small number of students who knew how the option worked but

**Table 3.11**

**Percentage of Respondents Unaware of the Option by Size of Anticipated Debt**

| Amount of Debt | Students from | |
|---|---|---|
| | Georgetown | Catholic |
| Low | 79% | 82% |
| High | 56% | 65% |
| Very High | 62% | 66% |

**Table 3.12**

**Source of Knowledge of Income-Contingent Repayment Option**

| Source of Knowledge | Students from | |
|---|---|---|
| | Georgetown (N=98) | Catholic (N=32) |
| Law School Career Services Office[a] | 10% | 13% |
| Newspaper or Magazine | 8% | 3% |
| U.S. Government Literature | 10% | 6% |
| Word of Mouth | 50% | 56% |
| Internet | 4% | 9% |
| Other | 17% | 13% |

[a]In designing the questionnaire, I should have included the financial aid office as a possible response to this question, since students trying to figure out how to balance their debts against their career decisions could receive advice from either law school office. However, even if all of the students who listed "other" in response to this option had received their information from the financial aid office, a majority would still have learned of it from word of mouth rather than from their law schools. In addition, it should be noted that the data in this table refer only to the approximately one-third of students who had heard of the option at all.

**Table 3.13**

**Intention to Use Income-Contingent Repayment Option among Students Having Heard of It**

| Intent to Use | Students from | |
|---|---|---|
| | Georgetown (N=97) | Catholic (N=32) |
| No, Because I Knew How it Worked but Decided Not to Use it | 24% | 13% |
| No, Because I Didn't Know Enough about it | 60% | 66% |
| Yes | 17% | 22% |

**Table 3.14**
**Reasons Georgetown Students with Sufficient Information Decided against Income-Contingent Repayment Option (N = 21)**

| Reason | Top Choice Given | Within Top 3 Choices |
|---|---|---|
| I Haven't Wanted to Agree to Long-term Indebtedness | 43% | 31% |
| I Don't Know What Jobs or Income I Will Have over a Long Period of Time, So it Has Been Difficult to Decide What Repayment Plan Would Be Best for Me in the Long Run | 14% | 28% |
| I'd Use this Plan If it Covered All My Loans, but I Need a High Income Because I Have Large Commercial Loans That Can't Be Consolidated into the Plan | 19% | 11% |
| The Total Payments Would Be Too High, Even If Some of the Money Were Eventually Forgiven | 5% | 13% |
| I Have Been Putting off until a Later Year My Planning of How I Will Repay My Loans | 14% | 11% |
| I Haven't Heard of Anyone Using this Program, So I Have Been Suspicious of It | 5% | 4% |
| LRAP Is Sufficient to Help Me Pay off My Loans | 0% | 0% |
| Other | 0% | 2% |

nevertheless had decided not to use it were asked the reasons for their decision. They were permitted to rank their reasons. Only the Georgetown database was large enough to produce a meaningful tabulation to this question.[17] Table 3.14 considers the first-ranked reasons and the top three reasons. It shows that the most important reasons, by far, are students' unwillingness to commit to a long repayment plan, the difficulty of long-term planning under conditions of uncertainty, and the fact that they had high private debts that would not be covered by income-contingent repayment.[18]

Because the number of students who had enough information to decide about income-contingent repayment was so low, I addressed further questions to respondents who already claimed to know about how income-contingency worked and had decided not to use it[19] and to the larger group of respondents who didn't have enough information about it.[20] I provided them with a description of the program, consisting of approximately one single-spaced page with the information about the regulations summarized in the second part of chapter 2 of this book. After they read a description of the program, they were asked whether they would probably want to use this option (see Table 3.15.) For the most part, this better-informed group still did not want to use income-

**Table 3.15**
**Probable Use of Income-Contingent Repayment Option by Students Desiring to Work in Public Interest Law and Informed about the Terms of the Option**

| Will you probably use this option? | Students from | |
|:---:|:---:|:---:|
| | Georgetown (N=238) | Catholic (N=91) |
| Yes | 20% | 39% |
| No | 80% | 61% |

contingent repayment, although the percentage interested at Catholic (which has no LRAP program) was twice as high as at Georgetown and is the most significant difference in the data supplied by students at the two schools.

This negative opinion of income-contingent repayment did not vary greatly among subgroups with larger debts. Among the Georgetown respondents, 17 percent of those with low and high debt said that they would use the option, while 21 percent of those with very high debt said that they would do so.

The students who had just been informed about the parameters of the program and had decided not to use it were then asked their reasons, just as those who had already known about the program had been asked earlier. The possible responses were similar to those offered in connection with the earlier question, but because these students had just been given detailed information about the option, I provided more specific explanatory wording for the reasons. The choices were as follows:

- "I don't want to be indebted for twenty-five years, even if the annual payments could be low and I might eventually get some forgiveness."

- "I don't know what jobs or income I will have over a long period of time, so it is difficult to decide what repayment plan would be best for me in the long run."

- "I'd use this plan if it covered all my loans, but I need a high income because I have large loans that can't be consolidated into the plan (they aren't government-guaranteed)."

- "The total payments would be too high because I expect my income to rise, and as my income rises, my payments will also rise, so little if any of my debt would be forgiven after twenty-five years."

- "The total payments would be too high, even if some of the money were forgiven after twenty-five years."

**Table 3.16**
**Reasons Students Who Had Just Been Informed about Income-Contingent Repayment Option Decided Not to Use This Option**

| Reason | Students from | | | |
|---|---|---|---|---|
| | Georgetown (N=188) | | Catholic (N=56) | |
| | Top Choice | Within Top 3 Choices | Top Choice | Within Top 3 Choices |
| Don't Want 25-Year Indebtedness Even with Low Payments and Possible Forgiveness | 50% | 30% | 45% | 31% |
| Difficult to Plan Long in Advance | 17% | 27% | 9% | 21% |
| Plan Doesn't Cover Commercial Debt | 19% | 16% | 20% | 17% |
| Expect Income to Rise | 5% | 10% | 13% | 12% |
| Total Payments Would Be Too High, Even with Forgiveness | 2% | 5% | 5% | 5% |
| Concerned about Tax in 25th Year | 1% | 1% | – | 3% |
| Putting off Planning | 2% | 5% | 2% | 3% |
| Haven't Heard of Anyone Using this Program | 1% | 2% | – | 1% |
| LRAP Is Sufficient | 2% | 1% | (No LRAP) | (No LRAP) |
| Other | 3% | 2% | 12% | 7% |

- "I would be worried about having to pay income tax on the amount forgiven in the twenty-fifth year."
- "I am putting off until a later year my planning of how I will repay my loans."
- "I haven't heard of anyone using this program, so I am suspicious of it."
- "LRAP is sufficient to help me pay off my loans." (Georgetown questionnaire only)
- Other

Table 3.16 reveals that the main reasons for reasonably well-informed public interest–oriented students' avoidance of the option are the same as those given by students who had not been so recently educated: the

**Table 3.17**

**Considerations in Georgetown Respondents' Decisions Not to Use Income-Contingent Repayment Option**

| Debt Level of Respondents | % Who Listed 25-Year Term as Primary Consideration | % Who Listed Commercial Debt as Primary Consideration |
|---|---|---|
| Low (N=13) | 61% | 8% |
| High (N=62) | 52% | 18% |
| Very High (N=113) | 48% | 20% |
| All Respondents | 50% | 19% |

*Note*: Respondents who listed considerations other than these were not included in this table, causing the total of percentages to be lower than 100 percent.

twenty-five-year commitment before forgiveness occurred,[21] the difficulty of deciding in favor of the option without knowing more about the student's future employment or income, and the plan's exclusion of commercial debt.

Unwillingness to sign up for a twenty-five-year repayment plan was, by far, the most important negative factor attributed to the income-contingent repayment plan. It should be noted, however, that as debt rose, the aversion to twenty-five-year repayment gave way, a bit, to non-coverage of commercial debt as a major factor against using income-contingent repayment. This result tends to suggest that as the percentage of students with very significant commercial debt rises (as it will each year that the annual ceiling on Stafford loans remains $18,500 despite increases in tuition and the cost of living), noncoverage of commercial debt will become a more important reason that students avoid the income-contingent repayment option. The Georgetown numbers are shown in Table 3.17.[22]

Finally, because I knew from talking with a few students while designing my questionnaire that aversion to twenty-five-year repayment would loom large as a reason for not considering an income-contingent plan,[23] I asked those students who had objected for this reason to clarify their objection.[24] Did they dislike twenty-five-year repayment because the term was simply too long in some absolute sense, or because the norm was ten-year repayment?[25] At both schools, a strong majority was averse simply because they could not bring themselves to sign up for a twenty-five-year term, but a significant minority (17 percent at Georgetown, 19 percent at Catholic) objected primarily because they did not want to deviate from the norm.

## NOTES

1. Georgetown's program is described in detail on its website, at http://www.law.georgetown.edu/finaid/lrap.html (last visited June 30, 2000).

2. Kate Ackley, *Til Debt Do Us Part*, LEGAL TIMES, Sept. 6, 1999, at S30.

3. For both Georgetown and Catholic Universities, the source of the data is AMERICAN BAR ASSOCIATION, APPROVED LAW SCHOOLS, 2000 EDITION (1999, reporting 1998–99 data), except that the data on average debt at graduation is derived from the schools' submissions to *U.S. News and World Report* and published at http://www.usnews.com/usnews/edu/beyond/grad/gradlaw.htm (last visited June 30, 2000). There are some slight discrepancies in the data reported to the ABA and the data reported to *U.S. News*, which could result from somewhat different methods of measurement. According to the *U.S. News and World Report* data, the tuition and fees at Georgetown were $25,705 and at Catholic, $25,092. *U.S. News and World Report* lists Georgetown's percentage of graduates in law firms at 72 percent, in business at 6 percent, in government at 8 percent, clerkships at 10 percent, and public interest jobs, 3 percent. It lists Catholic's equivalent percentages as 38 percent, 14 percent, 23 percent, 18 percent, and 2 percent.

4. A cover letter from a faculty member (myself at Georgetown, Professor Lisa Lerman at Catholic) explained that the survey would be used in connection with research about the federal income-contingent repayment option.

5. Both of these student organizations raise money for summer stipends for students who take summer jobs in public interest organizations.

6. The tuition and living expenses at the two schools are similar, but Georgetown students may be contributing a bit more to their expenses from family members, savings, or law firm summer jobs. Many Georgetown students (though relatively fewer of those with public interest aspirations) earn more than $15,000 by working for ten weeks after their second summer for one of the major law firms.

7. ROBERT V. STOVER, MAKING IT AND BREAKING IT: THE FATE OF PUBLIC INTEREST COMMITMENT DURING LAW SCHOOL (1989); David L. Chambers, *The Burdens of Educational Loans: The Impacts of Debt on Job Choice and Standards of Living for Students at Nine American Law Schools*, 42 J. LEGAL EDUC. 187 (1992); Lewis A. Kornhauser & Richard L. Revesz, *Legal Education and Entry into the Legal Profession: The Role of Race, Gender and Educational Debt*, 70 N.Y.U.L. REV. 829, 890 (1995).

8. Response on one Georgetown questionnaire.

9. Kornhauser & Revesz, *supra* note 7, at 957. *See also* Chambers, *supra* note 7, at 199. Kornhauser and Revesz's conclusions were based on data collected from 1987 through 1990 (and Chambers' data dated from 1989), when debt was much lower. However, even they concede that "debt affects an individual's decision making calculus as a constraint: an individual otherwise inclined to take a not-for-profit job will be deterred from doing so if her disposable income after taxes and debt-service payments is not greater, by some amount, than her living expenses as a student." Kornhauser & Revesz, *supra* note 7, at 890. Furthermore, they note that their conclusions "ought to be reexamined in the coming years [because] debt burdens are continuing to rise in real terms, and the effect of debt at one level may not be the same as that at a much higher level [and] debt might have a larger effect on career choice than it has now." *Id.* at 958.

10. Pay becomes a relatively more significant factor relative to debt as students move through law school. For the first-year Georgetown students, anticipated debt was a significant factor for 94 percent, and benefits were significant for 42 percent, but by the third year, these numbers were 84 percent and 56 percent. The Catholic students showed a similar trend. For first-year students, the numbers were debt, 91 percent, and benefits, 57 percent, but for third-year students, they were debt, 78 percent, and benefits, 68 percent. Students may have become more aware, as they moved through law school, of the huge gap between private sector and public sector pay, but debt remained the most commonly cited factor for not following a public interest career. For the Georgetown students, the frequency of mentioning debt did not vary appreciably according to whether the respondent was an EJF member, with 88 percent of EJF members and 91 percent of nonmembers mentioning debt, and 60 percent of members and 51 percent of nonmembers mentioning pay. For Catholic, the raw numbers were too low to make this comparison.

11. http://www.law.georgetown.edu/finaid/lrap.html#IIIA (last visited June 30, 2000).

12. Ibid.

13. "The United States Department of Education has a program (called the 'income-contingent repayment option') through which a graduating student can consolidate his or her government-guaranteed student loans into a single loan from the federal government and pay that consolidated loan back over a long period of time, with limited annual repayments. The repayments are tied by a formula to the income that the graduate received during the previous year. *Before* receiving this questionnaire, had you heard about this program?"

14. At Catholic, the percentage of those unaware had dropped to 47 percent by the third year, but there were only seventeen third-year respondents at Catholic, eight of whom had not heard of the option. The

apparent increase in awareness could be anomalous. Undergraduates are even less aware of the existence of the income-contingent repayment option. In a recent survey of students at 55 colleges, 86% of respondents were unfamiliar with the option. Tracey King and Ivan Frishberg, *Big Loans, Bigger Problems: A Report on the Sticker Shock of Student Loans* (2001), www.pirg.org/studentdebt/.

15. The number of respondents at Georgetown was large enough to investigate the degree of knowledge of the option from the most frequently relied upon sources. Among the forty-nine students who had learned of the program through word of mouth, only eight thought that they knew its terms, but among the ten who had learned of it from the U.S. government, seven thought that they knew its terms. Thus it may be that if the government did a better job of publicizing income-contingent repayment, students might learn more details of the program than they do from friends.

16. Neither Georgetown nor Catholic provided students with the option of borrowing their law student loans directly from the government, through direct lending, so consolidation would be needed to take advantage of income-contingent repayment through the direct lending program.

17. Only four Catholic students had made a deliberate decision not to use income-contingent repayment.

18. This conclusion equally applies to the subgroup of those with very high debt. Their top three reasons (aggregating their three top-ranked reasons) for not wanting to use income-contingency were avoiding long-term debt (30 percent), lack of information about their futures (27 percent), and lack of coverage of commercial loans (15 percent).

19. Students who thought that they knew about the program might have been misinformed about it, particularly since most of them knew about it through word of mouth. Therefore, I directed my summary of the program to these students as well as to those who admitted not knowing enough about it.

20. Thus, the only respondents not asked the remaining questions were the small number who had already decided to use income-contingent repayment.

21. The questionnaire made clear that the repayment plan could be switched to a different option, so that respondents would not necessarily lock themselves into twenty-five years of repayment. They were also made aware of the fact that forgiveness was not made available unless one remained in the plan for twenty-five years.

22. The number of Catholic respondents was too low to be meaningful.

23. As I was beginning to think about this book, I explained the income-contingent repayment plan to perhaps a dozen students, not all

of whom were at Catholic or Georgetown. I could see that they were interested until I mentioned that the repayment term was twenty-five years. At that point their eyes almost always became distant, and their interest became academic rather than personal. Several said that people in their mid-twenties could not be expected to sign any agreement that would affect their lives until they were in their fifties (as if their choices of law school, first jobs, and spouses didn't do so).

24. This question was directed to students who listed objection to a twenty-five-year term as one of their reasons, regardless of ranking.

25. The choice was either: "I wouldn't want to repay my student loans over such a long period even if twenty-five-year repayment becomes the norm for all law graduates, those going into the private and public sectors," or "I could accept repaying my student loans over such a long period if that were the norm for everyone, especially if that saved me some money. But I don't want to be making payments on my loans for fifteen years after most people I know have finished paying for school."

# 4

# Financial Aid Advisors

These surveys of students tend to show that there is relatively little interest in the income-contingent repayment option among students with high debts and low salary prospects, whether or not they are well-informed about its details. However, what about the professionals who advise these students about their financial obligations and opportunities? To learn something about their views on income-contingent repayment, I surveyed the law school financial aid advisors, sending a questionnaire by e-mail to all 153 law school financial aid advisors who listed an e-mail address either in their professional directory[1] or on their law school's website.[2] The advisors were able to complete the questionnaire without revealing their identities or law schools, and to those who did reveal their school names, I offered not to reveal the identities of individual respondents. Officials at ninety-eight law schools responded.[3]

According to the survey results, fifty-seven of the responding schools are private law schools. Twenty-five of those (as well as eight public law schools) have LRAP programs. Thirty of the schools (including seven of the fifty-seven private schools) participate in direct lending, making it possible for graduates to elect income-contingent repayment without first consolidating (and presumably making information about this option more readily available to them than at schools like Georgetown and Catholic). At about half of the responding law schools (52 percent), a majority of graduating students take their first jobs in large law firms (i.e., with more than 250 lawyers). At one third of the law schools, at least 10 percent of graduates start at salaries of $33,000 or less.

**Table 4.1**
**Financial Aid Advisors' Knowledge of the Option (N = 98)**

| Knowledge Level | % Respondents |
|---|---|
| Understood the Option Well (See Text) | 14% |
| Understood Basic Outline, but Not Familiar with Details | 62% |
| Had Heard of it, but Not Familiar with Basic Outline | 20% |
| Had Never Heard of it | 3% |

The actual cost of attending two-thirds of the responding schools exceeds the $18,500 annual Stafford loan limit; these schools are referred to as "high-tuition" schools for purposes of analyzing the questionnaire responses. Of the sixty-six schools in that category, twenty-nine have LRAP programs. Thirty-one percent of the schools reported that the average debt of their graduating students was $55,500 (three Stafford loans) or less; 59 percent, between $55,500 and $75,000; and 10 percent, more than $75,000. These categories are referred to for purposes of analysis as low-debt, high-debt, and very high-debt schools. Among the private schools, however, only 4 percent were low-debt schools, 78 percent were high-debt schools, and 18 percent were very high-debt schools.

I began by asking the financial aid advisors how much they knew about the federal income-contingent repayment option (see Table 4.1). Three percent had never heard of it. Twenty percent had heard of it but were not familiar with it. Sixty-two percent said that they understood "the basic outline of the option" but were "not familiar with it in detail." Advisors who checked this option might know enough about it to refer high-debt, low-income students to the government's website for further information. Only 14 percent said that they were familiar with its details.[4] To elect this option, they had to say that they understood "its repayment formulas, its limitation on capitalization of unpaid interest, the opportunities for entry into and exit from the option, and the forgiveness feature." In other words, they had to know enough about it (in the opinion of the author) to be able to offer expert advice to law students, including those who inquired about the option and those who might benefit from the option but had not previously heard about it.

I did not ask additional questions to the twenty-three financial aid advisors who had never heard of the income-contingent repayment option or who had heard of it but were not familiar with it. All of the remaining data was collected from the seventy-five advisors who at least understood the basic outlines of income-contingent repayment.

To find out what advice these advisors proffered, I asked what information about the income-contingent repayment option they or others in

**Table 4.2**
**Assistance Given by Financial Aid Advisors Familiar with Income-Contingent Repayment Option**

| | Advisors Who | | |
|---|---|---|---|
| Type of Assistance | Knew the Details (N=14) | Understood the Basic Outline (N=61) | All (N=75) |
| Help with Arithmetic, at Least by Request | 21% | 0% | 4% |
| Provide Printed Information or Explain How to Get it | 57% | 49% | 51% |
| Do Not Discuss Income-contingent Repayment Option | 21% | 51% | 45% |

*Note*: It could reasonably be assumed that the 23% of responding financial aid advisors who did not know even the general outlines of the program did not help students with the complex arithmetic. Thus, of the 98 advisors who responded to the survey, only 3 helped students to do the comparative computations.

their offices gave to students who expected to have low-income jobs but would graduate with high debt. Respondents had three choices:

- We do the income-contingent arithmetic with them (or at least with those who request us to do that), to help them decide whether this option would be helpful for them, either as a short-term option or over a twenty-five-year period.

- We tell them about the federal income-contingent option and give them printed information that is specifically about income-contingent repayment (or instructions about how to get specific information about this repayment plan), but we do not do the arithmetic with them as part of our counseling.

- We give them general information about loan repayment options (such as printed information about loan repayment choices or the Access Advisor diskette), but we do not usually discuss this specific option.

Consistent with the low degree of familiarity with the program's formulas, very few advisors or their offices assisted students with the quite complex arithmetic that is necessary to understand the comparative advantages and disadvantages of this repayment option. Table 4.2 displays the advice dispensed by all financial aid advisors who knew at least the basic outline of the program and by the fourteen who reported that they understood the option well.

Thus, nearly half of the advisors who know at least the outlines of the

**Table 4.3**

**Influence of Possible Factors on Type of Assistance Offered by the Most Knowledgeable Law School Financial Aid Advisors**

| Factor | Type of Assistance | |
|---|---|---|
| | Help with Arithmetic, Provide Printed Data, or Advise How to Get Information | Do Not Discuss Income-contingent Repayment Option |
| Knowledgeable Advisors | 55% | 45% |
| Advisors Who Believe That at Least 5% of Their Graduates Could Benefit in the Short or Long Term from the Option (N=35) | 66% | 34% |
| Advisors Who Believe That less than 5% of Their Graduates Could Benefit (N=33) | 45% | 55% |
| Private School (N=46) | 61% | 39% |
| Public School (N=29) | 45% | 55% |
| More than 10% of Graduates Take Low-paying Jobs ($33,000 or Less) (N=23) | 56% | 44% |
| Less than 10% of Graduates Take Low-paying Jobs (N=52) | 54% | 46% |
| School Participates in Federal Direct Lending (N=26) | 54% | 46% |
| School Does Not Participate in Direct Lending (N=49) | 55% | 45% |
| High-cost School (N=51)[a] | 61% | 39% |
| Low-cost School (N=24) | 42% | 58% |

[a]Cost of attendance exceeds annual Stafford limit.

income-contingent program do not inform students about it, and only 4 percent of them (all at private law schools) help with the math necessary to compare this method with other methods of repayment.

I performed some cross-tabulations to try to identify factors that might make it more likely that these advisors would discuss income-contingent repayment with law students. Because so few of them do the arithmetic with students, I divided the advisors into only two groups (see Table 4.3). Those in the first group either do the arithmetic, provide information, or inform students about how to get information. Members of the second group do not discuss income-contingent repayment at all.

The results suggest that neither a school's participation in direct lending nor the percentage of students who take very low-paying jobs has much influence on how much advice financial aid advisors provide about income-contingent repayment,[5] but the likelihood of providing at least minimal advice was increased if the advisor believed that a more substantial number of graduates could benefit from the program, if the school was a private school, or if the school was a high-cost school.

**Table 4.4**
**Opinions of the Most Knowledgeable Financial Aid Advisors about the Utility of the Income-Contingent Repayment Option for High-Debt, Low-Income Graduates (N = 75)**

| Opinion | % Holding View |
|---------|:--------------:|
| Many Might Benefit as a Long-Term Plan and Many Others for a Few Years | 39% |
| Benefit for a Few Years Only | 52% |
| Few If Any Would Benefit | 9% |

I sought to learn these advisors' opinions of the utility of income-contingent repayment by asking them to state their view of its use by their high-debt graduates "who want to work, at least for several years, in jobs that do not have high compensation (e.g., public interest, local government jobs, and very small firms)." I gave them three options for response:

- Many of these graduates might benefit by using it as a long-term repayment plan, and many others might benefit by using it for a few years and then switching to a more conventional repayment option.

- It would not be helpful as a long-term repayment plan for many of them, but a considerable number of them might benefit by using it for a few years and then switching to a more conventional repayment option.

- Very few, if any, of our graduates would benefit from either long-term or short-term use of this plan.

The overall responses are displayed in Table 4.4. They show that despite the advisors' lack of familiarity with the details of the program or their disinclination to help students compute whether it would be advantageous, the vast majority believe that the option would be useful for this segment of law graduates. Interestingly, the better the advisors knew the program, the less useful they thought it was, as indicated in Table 4.5.

Table 4.6 examines factors about their law schools that might influence the opinions of financial aid advisors about income-contingent repayment. Not surprisingly, advisors were more likely to think income-contingent repayment useful (especially for both long-term or short-term users) if their schools lacked an LRAP program, had more low-income graduates, and cost more to attend.

The eight advisors who didn't think that income-contingent repayment would be useful either for long-term or short-term use were asked to

**Table 4.5**
**Opinions about Utility as a Function of Greater Familiarity with the Plan**

| Opinion | % of Those Who Understood Details Very Well (N=14) | % of Those Who Understood the Basic Outline (N=61) |
|---|---|---|
| Many Might Benefit as a Long-term Plan and Many Others for a Few Years | 14% | 44% |
| Benefit for a Few Years Only | 64% | 49% |
| Few If Any Would Benefit | 21% | 7% |

**Table 4.6**
**Cross-Tabulation of Advisors' Opinions and Law School Characteristics**

| Law School Characteristic | Advisors Believing Plan Could Help High-debt, Low-Income Graduates Both in Long and Short Terms | Advisors Believing Plan Useful Only in Short Term | Advisors Believing Few If Any Graduates Would Benefit from Plan |
|---|---|---|---|
| All Respondents | 39% | 52% | 9% |
| School Has LRAP (N=33) | 29% | 61% | 11% |
| School Does Not Have LRAP (N=42) | 45% | 47% | 9% |
| More than 10% of Graduates Start at $33,000 or less (N=23) | 52% | 39% | 9% |
| Fewer than 10% of Graduates Start at $33,000 or less (N=52) | 32% | 58% | 10% |
| High-cost School (N=51) | 41% | 49% | 10% |
| Low-cost School (N=24) | 33% | 58% | 8% |

explain their reasoning. One did not respond. Table 4.7 summarizes the thinking of the other seven, although it should be noted that the number of respondents here is very low because so few thought the program useless.

A much larger group of forty respondents (including the eight who thought it not useful in either time frame) thought that income-contingent repayment would not help as a long-term repayment method. They were asked the reasons for their views about lack of long-term utility. They were offered eight possible explanations, as well as the opportunity to list an "other" reason. The eight options were these:

**Table 4.7**
**Reasons Given by the 7 Most Skeptical Advisors as to Why Income-Contingent Repayment Option Wouldn't Be Useful Even in the Short Term**

| Reason | Given as Top Reason | Given as Reason |
|---|---|---|
| Other, Less-complex, Repayment Plans Would Be Better for Those Who Can't Afford 10-Year Repayment | 43% (3 of 7) | 33% |
| Short-Term Users Don't Remain in the Program Long Enough to Qualify for Forgiveness and Will End up Paying More than on 10-Year Plan | 14% (1 of 7) | 28% |
| School's LRAP Program Is Sufficient | 29% (2 of 7) | 17% |
| Students Are Better off Working for Law Firms or Corporations to Reduce Debt Before Taking Low-paying Jobs | — | 11% |
| Department of Education Administration Is Unreliable | — | 6% |
| Other | 14% (1 of 7) | 6% |

- It only covers governmentally extended and government-guaranteed debt.
- It requires twenty-five-year amortization to qualify for forgiveness, and such a long repayment period is too long for our graduates, even if the financial terms (including eventual forgiveness) were advantageous.
- Few graduates will remain in the program long enough to qualify for forgiveness, and they will end up paying more money than if they elected a more traditional repayment plan.
- The program is useful only to those high-debt students who can predict what their career paths will be and know that they will have low incomes for a long time, but few if any of our graduates will fit that profile.
- The forgiveness eventually offered by the program is taxable as income.
- I have not yet heard of law graduates benefitting by using this program.
- This school has a Loan Repayment Assistance Program, and it is sufficient to meet the needs of most of our high-debt, low-income graduates.
- Administration by the Department of Education, either of direct lending generally or of this option, is unreliable.

**Table 4.8**

**For Financial Aid Advisors Who Believe Income-Contingent Repayment Would Not Be a Useful Long-Term (25-Year) Option, Reasons For That Opinion (N = 40)**

| Reason | Given as Top Reason | Given as Reason |
|---|---|---|
| Doesn't Cover Commercial Debt | 5% | 14% |
| 25 Years Is Too Long, Even If Forgiveness Would Be Advantageous | 13% | 14% |
| Few Graduates Will Remain in the Program Long Enough to Obtain Forgiveness, and They Will Pay Too Much Compared to Standard Repayment | 40% | 26% |
| Long-term Career Paths Are Too Unpredictable | 15% | 16% |
| Forgiveness Is Taxable | 7% | 8% |
| I Haven't Heard of Others Using it | 7% | 9% |
| LRAP Is Sufficient | 10% | 9% |
| Department of Education Administration Is Unreliable | 0% | 3% |
| Other | 3% | 1% |

As Table 4.8 shows, a plurality of them believed that few graduates would remain in the program long enough to qualify for forgiveness and would end up paying too much money.

Finally, I asked the financial aid advisors who had been familiar with income-contingent repayment to estimate the percentage of their students who would benefit by using it and the percentage who actually did use it. Apparently, schools do not usually ask their graduates to report back to them on the repayment method they elect, for 80 percent of the advisors stated that they would have no way of making even a rough estimate of the percentage who actually used the option.[6] Table 4.9 shows that an overwhelming majority of the advisors (86 percent) nevertheless believes that at least 1 percent of their schools' graduates would benefit, and a majority (52 percent) believes that the percentage is more than 5 percent. Contrast these percentages with the mere 4 percent of advisors who help their students, even when requested, with the arithmetic needed to evaluate the utility of income-contingent repayment.

Not surprisingly, the percentage of advisors who thought that at least 5 percent of students would benefit was higher at private schools (60 percent) than at public schools (37 percent), higher at schools lacking an

**Table 4.9**
**Estimates by Financial Aid Advisors Familiar with Income-Contingent Repayment Option of the Percentage of Their Schools' Graduates Who Would Benefit (N = 68)**

| Estimate | % Respondents |
|---|---|
| More than 10% | 25% |
| 5%–10% | 27% |
| 1%–4.9% | 34% |
| Fewer than 1% | 11% |
| None | 3% |

LRAP program (55 percent) than at those that had such programs (46 percent), higher at schools where at least 10 percent of graduates took low-paying jobs (70 percent) than at those where fewer took such jobs (43 percent), and higher at high-cost schools (54 percent) than at low-cost schools (45 percent). The data also showed that the advisors who reported understanding the details of the income-contingent plan were less likely to believe that at least 5 percent would benefit (36 percent), compared to those advisors who only knew its general outlines (55 percent). This finding seems consistent, however, with the earlier conclusion that the advisors who best understood the plan were less likely to think that it was beneficial to students.[7]

## NOTES

1. LAW SCHOOL ADMISSION COUNCIL, DIRECTORY, 1998–99 (1999).

2. The American Bar Association accredits 182 law schools, but not all have financial aid advisors, and not all financial aid officers list e-mail addresses. Some of those who do list addresses and were included in my survey are not technically law school advisors and do not actually have offices in their law school. These officials work in a central university administration office and are the primary persons designated to answer questions from law students, but they do not see law students on a daily basis as the financial aid advisors situated in law schools inevitably do. In a few instances, the officials who received my inquiries did not respond, and I followed up by asking Georgetown's financial aid advisor to give them additional copies of my questionnaire at their annual convention.

3. This absolute number of responses is, of course, small, but the data might be fairly representative because it represents more than half of all U.S. law schools.

4. This percentage rose to 19 percent among financial aid advisors at private law schools, the schools whose students have more substantial debt. However, it was only 15 percent among financial aid advisors at schools at which more than 10 percent of the graduates start at salaries of $33,000 or less. It fell to 10 percent among advisors at the twenty-nine schools where the average debt of graduates was less than $55,500.

5. It should be noted, however, that these results are displayed only for advisors who knew at least the basic outlines of income-contingent repayment, and that direct lending participants were somewhat more likely (87 percent compared to 72 percent) to fall into that category.

6. Of the fifteen who were able to estimate, two said none; four said fewer than 1 percent, seven said 1 to 4 percent, one said 5 to 10 percent, and one said more than 10 percent.

7. See Table 4.5.

# 5

# Is Income-Contingent Repayment Good for You?

Chapter 2 of this book reported the high hopes of Congress and President Clinton that income-contingent repayment would help to enable idealistic students, including law students, to enter public service. But the survey data in chapters 3 and 4 suggest a dismal image of the utility of income-contingent repayment for idealistic law graduates. Half of the students who want to spend at least one-third of their careers in public service do not expect to do so, and at least 90 percent of those students cite their student debt as a significant reason for forgoing the opportunity. Approximately two-thirds of these students have never heard of the income-contingent repayment option, and only 9 percent even know generally what it provides. Among the very few who know about it, only about one-fifth plan to use it. When informed about the details of the option, only one-fifth to two-fifths of the students wanted to use it. Professional financial aid advisors are slightly better informed but at least as skeptical. Only 14 percent of them understand the option well. Half of the advisors who know of the program at least generally think that it would benefit at least 5 percent of their students, and a quarter think that it would help more than 10 percent of their students. But only 4 percent go over the complex arithmetic with the students whom it could help, even on request, and nearly half don't discuss it with students at all.

This skepticism and lack of knowledge on the part of both students and advisors would be justified or at least harmless if the income-contingent repayment option is so poor that in fact only an infinitesimal

fraction of high-debt, low-income students would be advantaged by using it. To evaluate its utility generally, and to enable law students to
compare how their own debts would fare under income-contingent repayment and other repayment plans, my research assistant Tai-yeu Hsia
and I constructed an interactive income-contingent loan repayment calculator. FinAid, a public interest website for information on student
loans, has made an HTML version of this calculator available without
charge.[1]

A person using this website calculator enters, in specified fields, his
or her government-guaranteed debts that are eligible for consolidation
in the direct lending program,[2] the applicable interest rate or rates, his
or her starting income (including any spousal income), and the anticipated rate of income growth.[3] Guessing future income growth is one of
the more difficult aspects of using the calculator, but one can ask prospective employers about their historical rate of salary increases, and one
can also make alternative assumptions about future income growth and
test them. The user of the calculator may also assume a sudden increase
in his or her future income level (e.g., a change from public interest to
law firm employment). Finally, the user may enter the current thirty-
year government bond rate (or a different discount rate, if preferred) to
reflect the financial advantage of repaying money later rather than
sooner.[4]

The calculator will then provide the user with the monthly payment
for the first month and every month until the debt is paid off or forgiven;
the time at which the debt will be paid off or forgiven; the total of payments that the student will pay over time; the amount of the debt that
the government will forgive as a result of the subsidies built into the
option; and the projected principal balance at the end of every month
(which will help the user to decide whether to prepay the debt or switch,
at any given point, to 10-year or some other form of repayment).[5] The
calculator will also show the present value of the stream of future repayments and of any amount of subsidy that the government will eventually provide. Because the value of a dollar paid twenty-five years from
now is less than the value of a dollar paid ten years from now, only
present value calculations can enable a borrower to compare the cost of
repayment using two or more repayment plans with different terms.[6]

The FinAid website also allows a borrower to compare income-
contingent repayment with ten-year repayment, thirty-year "extended"
repayment, or repayment over any other number of years. Similar calculators are available on other sites,[7] but this one uniquely computes
present value so that the cost of a loan paid under one of these methods
can more accurately be compared to the cost of income-contingent repayment.

**Table 5.1**

**Characteristics of Income-Contingent Repayment Option for "Larry Lifer" ($75,500 Debt, $32,000 Starting Salary)**

| Selected Repayment Characteristics | Income Increases at | | |
|---|---|---|---|
| | 2% | 3% | 4% |
| Monthly Payments, Year 1[a] | $394 | $394 | $394 |
| Monthly Payments, Year 6 | $428 | $457 | $488 |
| Total Payments (Current Dollars) | $144,107 | $171,440 | $194,477 |
| Present Value of Total Future Payments | $73,677 | $84,444 | $94,272 |
| Amount the Government Forgives (Current Dollars) | $100,845 | $71,427 | $29,543 |
| Present Value of Government Forgiveness | $24,633 | $17,447 | $7,216 |

[a]Because the income-contingent repayment option only permits consolidation of government-guaranteed debt, repayment of any further commercial debt must be added to the monthly figures.

## LARRY AND LISA LIFER, PUBLIC INTEREST CAREERISTS

With the calculator in hand, consider the situation of Larry Lifer, a law student graduating in June 2000[8] with $15,000 in government-guaranteed undergraduate debt, $55,500 in additional debt as a result of law school Stafford loans, and $5,000 in accrued interest from the law school loans.[9] If he consolidates his loans into a federal direct loan now, the loan will bear an annual interest rate of 8.25 percent.[10] Mr. Lifer has been offered a position as a staff attorney in a neighborhood legal services office in the continental United States at the typical starting salary of $32,000. He plans to spend his entire career in legal services work. He is not married. Because legal services budgets depend on an annual funding process and his office does not have a fixed or unionized salary scale, he and his future employer are a little uncertain about the rate of salary increase that he can expect. It might be 2 percent, 3 percent, or 4 percent. Let us say that the thirty-year bond rate is currently 5.8 percent.

Table 5.1 shows the important characteristics of repayment for the three assumptions about the rate of salary increase. It shows that in all of these cases, payments in the first year and the sixth year are much lower than the $926 required by ten-year repayment. Thus, the main goal of income-contingent repayment, keeping payments affordable, is met. In addition, the government provides additional loan subsidies for borrowers at all of these levels of increasing income, but the degree of subsidy is highly sensitive to the rate of increase. If Mr. Lifer's income increases at 2 percent per year, the government will write off about 24 percent of the total debt repayment (measured in terms of present value). If his income increases by 4 percent annually, the government will write off only about 7 percent of the debt.

Income-contingent repayment could be attractive to Larry Lifer at all three of these rates of salary increases, because it is a way to keep payments low in relation to income. Indeed, recalling the very highest percentage of income (20 percent, twice as high as the government's own recommendation) that professionals have recommended as a ceiling for student debt,[11] income-contingent repayment is the only way to make repayment affordable, particularly in the early years (see Table 5.2). Among repayment plans that reduce payments (compared to standard ten-year repayment), it may even be a good way to keep down the total amount paid, because it most greatly reduces payment right away while keeping total payments over the life of the loan comparable to other payment-reduction plans. As noted, however, Mr. Lifer's federal subsidy is not very great if he will experience income increases as large as 4 percent annually.

What if Mr. Lifer is unduly pessimistic, and he actually achieves 5 percent or 7 percent salary increases after electing the income-contingent repayment option? He will obtain no subsidy, because he will pay off his loan before he gets to the twenty-five-year mark, but that doesn't necessarily spell disaster. He can switch to ten-year repayment when he can afford it, or he can keep paying through the income-contingent plan, taking note of the comparisons in Table 5.3. Note that even under the most expensive version of income-contingent repayment (5 percent income increases), Mr. Lifer will pay only about $16,000 more, in terms of present value, than his fellow graduate who pays the loan over ten years.

Of course, as he is electing how to pay his debts, Mr. Lifer will be very eager to know what his rate of income increase is likely to be, because although he will on the whole be better off if it is higher, he will be more heavily subsidized if the rate is lower. It may not be easy for him to get this information, but he could start by asking his future employer for projections or at least historical figures on the rate of increase. For a very rough estimate, he could consult Table 5.4, the results of an unscientific survey of civil legal aid offices. This table was constructed because although all law school career services offices know the starting salaries at a large range of legal aid and other public interest employers, there seems to be no published compilation of the rates of projected or historical salary increase at such institutions. For purposes of assessing the utility to law graduates of income-contingent repayment, the national average (the mean) for such programs is not necessary, but

**Table 5.2**

**Comparison of Repayment Plans for "Larry Lifer" with 4% Increases**

| Selected Repayment Characteristics | Standard Repayment | Graduated Repayment (Debt Repaid in 30 Years) | Extended 30-Year Repayment | Extended 25-Year Repayment | Income-contingent Repayment Option with 4% Income Increases |
|---|---|---|---|---|---|
| Monthly Payments, Year 1 (% of After-tax Income[a]) | $926 (41%) | $519 (23%) | $567 (25%) | $595 (26%) | $394 (17%) |
| Monthly Payments, Year 6 (% of After-tax Income, Based on Gross Income of $40,500[b]) | $926 (34%) | $540 (20%) | $567 (21%) | $595 (22%) | $488 (22%) |
| Total Payments (Current Dollars) | $111,123 | $216,364 | $204,195 | $178,584 | $194,477 |
| Present Value of Total Future Payments | $84,738 | $98,175 | $94,605 | $94,170 | $94,272 |
| Amount the Government Forgives (Current Dollars) | 0 | 0 | 0 | 0 | $29,543 |
| Present Value of Government Forgiveness | 0 | 0 | 0 | 0 | $7,216 |

*Note*: Under the federal government's graduated repayment plan, the period within which the debt is scheduled for repayment increases as the amount of the debt goes up. For a $75,500 debt, the period is up to thirty years. Unlike thirty-year extended payment, however, the amount of monthly repayment is not steady. It starts at a smaller level in the early years, and increases over the period of repayment, on the assumption that the borrower's income will rise. A borrower can choose a period of repayment shorter than the maximum. I would have preferred to compare twenty-five-year graduated repayment with twenty-five-year income-contingent repayment, but neither the government's website calculator nor, apparently, any other online calculator permit the user to assume a repayment period shorter than the maximum. The data on graduated repayment in this chart were calculated on the government's web site, http://www.ed.gov/offices/OSFAP/DirectLoan/RepaytCalc/dlentry2.html.

[a]Assumes a personal exemption of $4,300, a standard deduction of $2,750, federal income tax of $3,746 and state and local incomes taxes of $1,124 (30% of federal tax). The personal exemptions, standard deductions and tax rates in this book are based on 1999 rules. Internal Revenue Service, Pub. 17 (1999).

[b]Assumes $6,026 in federal tax and $1,807 in state and local tax.

**Table 5.3**

Comparison of Six Repayment Plans, Including Three Assumptions about Income Increases under an Income-Contingent Repayment Plan

| Selected Repayment Characteristics | Standard Repayment | Graduated Repayment (30 Years[a]) | Extended Repayment (30 Years) | Income-contingent Repayment (3% Increases) | Income-contingent Repayment (5% Increases, Debt Paid in 24.4 Years) | Income-contingent Repayment (7% Increases, Debt Paid in 19.4 Years) |
|---|---|---|---|---|---|---|
| Monthly Payments, Year 1 | $926 | $519 | $567 | $394 | $394 | $394 |
| Monthly Payments, Year 6 | $926 | $540 | $567 | $457 | $519 | $586 |
| Total Payments (Current Dollars) | $111,123 | $216,364 | $204,195 | $171,440 | $200,439 | $170,711 |
| Present Value of Total Future Payments | $84,738 | $98,175 | $94,605 | $84,444 | $99,109 | $95,429 |
| Amount the Government Forgives (Current Dollars) | 0 | 0 | 0 | $71,427 | 0 | 0 |
| Present Value of Government Forgiveness | 0 | 0 | 0 | $17,477 | 0 | 0 |

[a]See Table 5.2, note.

**Table 5.4**
**Starting Salaries at Civil Legal Aid Offices (N = 51)**

| Starting Salary | % (No.) of Programs |
| --- | --- |
| $25,000–$27,000 | 25% (13) |
| $27,001–$29,000 | 10% (5) |
| $29,001–$31,000 | 33% (17) |
| $31,001–$33,000 | 10% (5) |
| More than $33,000 | 22% (11) |

the range of possibilities is worth knowing. Therefore, a true random sample was unnecessary and was in any event beyond the scope of this project. The data was collected by asking Don Saunders, an official of the National Legal Aid and Defenders Association, to suggest individual legal aid office directors who would be most likely respond to a survey on their salary practices. I sent questionnaires to ninety-five individuals whom he suggested, and I received fifty-one replies.

My first question asked for the organization's starting salary. The responses indicate that although $32,000 may be the national average starting salary for these jobs,[12] many legal services offices start at a lower level, some of them as low as $25,000 to $25,500 (reported by six offices). I also asked these directors to provide historical or estimated data on the rate of salary increases for the first ten years of an attorney's career with the office and for the following ten years. Some of them wrote letters to me about the difficulty of providing this data:

- "The percentage of salary increase was difficult to estimate because of our continuing uncertainty regarding federal funding. Our Board, for several years, was simply giving end of the year bonuses to deal with the funding uncertainty."[13]

- "Since our salary figures vary each year, and in some years when funding has been particularly tight, our staff have not received salary increases at all, it is difficult to estimate the increases in a % fashion. Normally our attorney staff receive less than a thousand dollars in salary increase each year."[14]

- "[T]here is little predictability in our salaries. . . . When funding declines, as it often does, we sometimes freeze salaries. Then we may give a relatively large increase to catch up. . . . Our increases tend to be in dollar amounts rather than percentages; i.e., attorneys will get a $1500 increase rather than a 3 percent increase. This practice . . . means that as a percentage, increases are often less each year."[15]

**Table 5.5**
**Reported Rates of Annual Salary Increases for Legal Aid Lawyers During First Decade of Practice (N = 50)**

| Rate of Increase | % (No.) of Programs |
|:---:|:---:|
| 2% | 4% (2) |
| 3% | 18% (9) |
| 4% | 22% (11) |
| 5% | 32% (16) |
| 6% or More | 24% (12) |

The reported rates of increase during the first ten years fell into the pattern shown in Table 5.5.

Because so many programs had starting salaries substantially below the national mean, I looked particularly at the rates of increase during the first ten years for the group of programs that started lawyers at $27,000 or less (see Table 5.6). These rates varied from 2 percent (one program) through 3 percent (three programs)[16] up to 10 percent (one program). I therefore ran a set of income-contingent repayment calculations assuming a lower-than-average starting salary of $27,000, at various rates of increase, for "Lisa Lifer."

As this table indicates, for a person starting at the low end of the salary scale, even a 4 percent annual rate of increased income results in a very substantial federal subsidy, which in terms of present value is almost 20 percent of the debt repayment. However, high rates of salary increase do require larger total repayment, and a borrower experiencing rapid income increases might at some point convert to a different repayment plan. For example, if Ms. Lifer's actual increases were 7 percent, her debt would have grown to $86,272, including the accrued but uncapitalized interest that she owed the government, by the beginning of the sixth year. If she calculated the consequences of shifting at that point to standard ten-year repayment, she would discover that such a conversion would require her to repay only $126,978 (in current dollars) over the remaining loan period, rather than $167,790 if she remained in income-contingent repayment. In terms of present value, she would have to expend only about $97,000, rather than $110,000 through income-contingent repayment. But her monthly payments in the sixth year would suddenly increase from $492 (18 percent based on one-twelfth of her after-tax income of $32,687)[17] to $1,058 (37 percent). This much more rapid payment may simply not be affordable.

It should be noted that the calculator and the tables are premised on a constant rate of salary increase, set by the borrower to estimate the value of income-contingent repayment. Similarly, the government's cal-

**Table 5.6**
**Characteristics of Income-Contingent Repayment Option for "Lisa Lifer"**
**($75,500 Debt, $27,000 Starting Salary)**

| Selected Repayment Characteristics | Income Increases at | | | |
|---|---|---|---|---|
| | 2% | 4% | 7% (Debt Repaid in 24.9 Years) | 10% (Debt Repaid in 19.2 Years) |
| Monthly Payments, Year 1 | $311 | $311 | $311 | $311 |
| Monthly Payments, Year 6 | $336 | $386 | $470 | $563 |
| Total Payments (Current Dollars) | $112,076 | $161,635 | $211,050 | $175,525 |
| Present Value of Total Future Payments | $57,492 | $76,879 | $99,333 | $96,139 |
| Amount the Government Forgives (Current Dollars) | $133,476 | $83,908 | 0 | 0 |
| Present Value of Government Forgiveness | $32,603 | $20,496 | 0 | 0 |

culator assumes a constant rate of income increase, although the rate on that calculator is set inflexibly at 5 percent. However, as one legal services director noted in his letter, the rate of increase may actually drop, so the tables and the calculator may understate the value of income-contingent repayment. In fact, eighteen of the fifty-one programs reported decreasing percentages of salary raises, and none reported accelerating percentages of increases. The programs with the lowest rate of initial increase (under 5 percent) reported the smallest drop (to 4 percent after ten years). Those with rates of increase of 5 percent to 7 percent tended to drop them by 2 percent, while those with the largest initial increases, in the range of 8 percent to 10 percent, tended to drop the rate by as much as 5 percent after a decade, unless the attorney was promoted to a managerial position.

## RALPH REFORMER, TEST-CASE LITIGATOR

Suppose Larry Lifer's classmate Ralph Reformer undertakes a career, not in a legal services office starting at $27,000 or $32,000 with 3 percent increases, but in a public interest law firm devoted to test-case litigation, public policy education, or public interest lobbying. To learn what I could about starting salaries and rates of increases at the much smaller number of these organizations, I sent out a survey to fifteen of their directors.[18] I received six replies, which are displayed in Table 5.7.

Suppose that Mr. Reformer spends his career at firm number 4, about

**Table 5.7**
**Starting Salaries and Rates of Salary Increase in Public Interest Law Firms**

| Firm No. | Years Experience Required of Starting Lawyers | Starting Salary | Rate of Salary Increase, First 10 Years | Rate of Salary Increase, Second 10 Years | No. Lawyers Employed |
|---|---|---|---|---|---|
| 1 | 0 | $31,300 | 3% | 3% | More than 15 |
| 2 | At Least 3 | $35,000 | 6% | 4% | 6–15 |
| 3 | 4 | $36,750 | 8.5% | 4% | 5 or Fewer |
| 4 | 1 | $38,000 | 4.5% | 4% | More than 15 |
| 5 | 4 | $41,000 | 5% | 2% | 6–15 |
| 6 | 5 | $50,000 | At Least as Much as Inflation | Same | 6–15 |

halfway through this list. In that case, his repayment options are sum-marized in Table 5.8. This table suggests a surprising conclusion. One might think that income-contingent repayment would have few attrac-tions for someone starting with income as high as $38,000. Yet the early-year payments on this plan are far more affordable than those under ten-year repayment, for even in the sixth year, standard repayment would consume nearly a third of after-tax income. Although all non-standard repayment plans are more costly in the long run than ten-year repayment, the thirty-year graduated and twenty-five-year extended repayment plans will cost the borrower more over time than will income-contingent repayment.

## CINDY CIVIC, SERVING THE POOR FIRST AND GETTING RICH LATER

Unlike Larry and Lisa Lifer, Cindy Civic does not think of herself as committed to a life of public interest law. She expects that eventually, she will follow many of her classmates into a fairly large law firm, where her income will be well above $100,000 per year. For four or five years, how-ever, she wants to work in a public interest job, either because she consid-ers it her public duty to serve people who are less fortunate than she, or because she thinks that public service work will be more fun than law firm work and she wants to undertake it before she has children to support.

Ms. Civic therefore plans four years of work with Lisa Lifer in her legal services office. At the beginning of her fifth year, she imagines that she will have a dramatic career shift, going to work for a corporate law

**Table 5.8**
**Repayment Options for "Ralph Reformer," an Attorney at a Public Interest Law Firm ($75,500 Debt, at Public Interest Law Firm No. 4, Starting Salary $38,000, with 4.5% Increases)**

| Selected Repayment Characteristics | Income-contingent Repayment (Debt Repaid in 18.6 Years) | Standard Repayment | Graduated Repayment (Debt Repaid in 30 Years[a]) | Extended 25-Year Repayment |
|---|---|---|---|---|
| Monthly Payments, Year 1 (Payment as a % of Taxable Income[b]) | $494 (19%) | $926 (36%) | $519 (20%) | $596 (23%) |
| Monthly Payments, Year 6 (Payment as a % of Taxable Income[c]) | $628 (20%) | $926 (29%) | $541 (17%) | $596 (19%) |
| Total Payments (Current Dollars) | $159,095 | $111,123 | $216,364 | $178,584 |
| Present Value of Total Future Payments | $93,554 | $84,738 | $98,175 | $95,526 |

[a]See Table 5.2, NOTE.
[b]The assumptions as to after tax-income are that this single taxpayer will pay $5,354 in federal income tax (as provided by the 1999 tax table) and another $1,606 in state and local income tax.
[c]The borrower's gross income will have risen to $49,486, and taxable income to $42,436, assuming a standard deduction. Federal tax is assumed to be $8,532, and state and local tax $2,560, keeping it in the same ratio to federal tax as in the previous calculation.

firm at a salary of $150,000, not nearly as high as what she would be making if she had started at the firm immediately after law school, but a conservative estimate and one worth settling for in order to have the privilege of doing for four years the full-time service work that she always wanted to undertake.

Like Lisa Lifer, Ms. Civic has $75,500 of government-guaranteed debt and will start her professional life with a salary of $27,000, and she will obtain raises of 4 percent annually before she changes jobs. After her change, her new $150,000 salary will continue to rise by 4 percent per year.

How will Ms. Civic manage those first four years? She cannot elect standard repayment at the outset, because the $926 monthly payments would amount to 46 percent of her after-tax income.[19] Income-contingent repayment would reduce those payments to $311, only 18 percent of her income. What would happen if she remained in the income-contingent repayment plan until the debt were repaid? Table 5.9 provides the answer.

This table shows that if Ms. Civic's primary debt repayment goal is to

**Table 5.9**
Repayment Options for "Cindy Civic," a Legal Aid Lawyer Who Joins a Corporate Law Firm after 5 Years (Debt $75,000, Initial Salary $27,000, Raises at 4%, New Job at $150,000 after 4 Years, with Further Raises at 4%)

| Selected Repayment Characteristics | Standard Repayment (Shown for Comparison, but Impossible Because Ms. Civic Can't Afford the Initial Payments) | Remain in Income-contingent Repayment until Debt Is Paid (12.5 Years in All) | 5 Years of Income-contingent Repayment, Followed by Conversion of the Remaining Debt to 10 More Years Standard Repayment | 5 Years of Income-contingent Repayment, Followed by Level Payment of the Remaining Debt in 5 More Years |
|---|---|---|---|---|
| Monthly Payments, Year 1 (% of After-tax Income) | $926 (46%) | $311 (16%) | $311 (16%) | $311 (16%) |
| Monthly Payments, Year 6[a] (% of After-tax Income[b]) | $926 (12%) | $1,304 (16%) | $1,077 (14%) | $1,791 (23%) |
| Total Payments (Current Dollars) | $111,123 | $138,258 | $149,948 | $128,161 |
| Present Value of Total Future Payments | $84,738 | $90,184 | —[c] | — |

[a]If Ms. Civic were to remain in income-contingent repayment, she would not make higher payments on her fifth-year much-increased salary until the beginning of the sixth year.

[b]Assumes (somewhat unrealisticallly) that Ms. Civic is still taking the standard deduction. She will have a gross income of $150,000, federal tax of $42,356, and state tax of $13,068.

[c]Not easily calculable.

keep monthly payments at the lowest possible percentage (14 percent) of her monthly after-tax income after she takes her law firm job, her best strategy would be to convert to standard ten-year repayment shortly after her career change makes it possible to make higher payments. She would pay off the debt in a total of fifteen years. However, at her new, high salary, she may be able to afford paying 16 percent of her after-tax income toward her student debt. If so, she would actually be better off remaining in income-contingent repayment until the debt is paid off in a total of twelve and one-half rather than fifteen years. On the other hand, she might prefer to pay off the remaining debt quite rapidly, over a five-year period, after she changes jobs. If so, she will have to pay 23 percent of her after-tax income toward her debt repayment in the sixth year to pay off the debt in a total of ten years.[20]

## FAY FEDERAL, JUSTICE DEPARTMENT LAWYER

Suppose that Fay Federal enters the U.S. Department of Justice in its Honors Program and works at the Department's headquarters in Washington, D.C. She will enter at the GS-11 level, which in the year 2000 started at $42,724 with 3 percent annual raises.[21] Her options would look like Table 5.10, and any repayment program other than standard repayment is plausible.

## MAX MERGER, CORPORATE LAWYER

Finally, a reader of this book might be curious about the utility of income-contingent repayment for graduates with high debts who are planning to work for corporate law firms with high starting salaries and rapid rates of advancement. Table 5.11 shows that Max Merger, a typical corporate lawyer, starting at $75,000 and expecting 10 percent raises, would actually repay a little less using the income-contingent repayment option than using a standard ten-year level repayment schedule. The reason for this is that the government's income-contingent repayment formula would require a graduate with such a high income to repay a larger percentage of that income (as well as a larger amount), and as a result, the graduate using this plan would pay off the debt in seven and one-half years rather than ten years. (Mr. Merger, on the other hand, might prefer to pay off his student loan over a very long term, using his high income for investments rather than loan repayments).[22]

It should be clear from these tables that neither the income-contingent repayment calculator nor a table comparing income-contingent repayment with other repayment options can dictate which system a borrower

**Table 5.10**

**Comparison of Repayment Plans for "Fay Federal," a Justice Department Lawyer (Debt of $75,500, Starting Income of $42,724, with 3% Increases)**

| Selected Repayment Characteristics | Standard Repayment | Graduated Repayment (Debt Repaid in 30 Years[a]) | Extended 25-Year Repayment | Income-contingent Repayment (Debt Repaid in 17.3 Years) |
|---|---|---|---|---|
| Monthly Payments, Year 1 (% of After-tax Income[b]) | $926 (33%) | $519 (18%) | $595 (22%) | $573 (20%) |
| Monthly Payments, Year 6 (% of After-tax Income, Based on Gross Income of $49,845[c]) | $926 (29%) | $540 (17%) | $595 (18%) | $664 (21%) |
| Total Payment (Current Dollars) | $111,123 | $216,364 | $178,584 | $148,552 |
| Present Value of Total Future Payments | $84,738 | $98,175 | $88,006 | $91,785 |

[a]See table 5.2, NOTE.

[b]Assumes federal income tax of $6,642 and state and local income taxes of $1,993.

[c]Assumes federal tax of $8,630 and state and local tax of $2,589.

Table 5.11

Comparison of Repayment Plans for "Max Merger," a Lawyer in a Corporate Firm (Debt of $75,000, Starting Income of $75,500, with 10% Increases)

| Selected Repayment Characteristics | Standard Repayment | Graduated Repayment (Debt Repaid in 30 Years[a]) | Extended 25-Year Repayment | Income-contingent Repayment (Debt Repaid in 7.7 Years) |
|---|---|---|---|---|
| Monthly Payments, Year 1 (% of After-tax Income[b]) | $926 (22%) | $519 (12%) | $595 (13%) | $1,040 (25%) |
| Monthly Payments, Year 6 (% of After-tax Income, Based on Gross Income of $132,867[c]) | $926 (12%) | $540 (7%) | $595 (8%) | $1,184 (16%) |
| Total Payments (Current Dollars) | $111,123 | $216,364 | $178,583 | $102,732 |
| Present Value of Total Future Payments | $84,738 | $98,175 | $95,526 | $82,886 |

[a]See Table 5.2, NOTES.
[b]Assumes federal income tax of $15,851 and state and local income taxes of $4,755.
[c]Assumes federal tax of $33,783 and state and local tax of $10,134.

should use. Each individual must decide, based on the individual's own circumstances, whether income-contingent repayment is desirable. For a high-debt, low-income borrower, the income-contingent repayment plan is a strong tool for lowering debt repayment. In addition, lawyers who start at very low salaries, or who expect very low rates of salary increase, and particularly those lawyers who start at a low rate *and* expect a low rate of increase, will benefit not only by lowering their payments but also by obtaining substantial federal subsidies. In addition, although the current-dollar cost of using income-contingent repayment appears much higher than the current-dollar cost of ten-year repayment, the present values of the future streams of payments are sometimes remarkably similar. High-debt, high-income borrowers might also consider income-contingent repayment as a method for paying off their debts even more quickly than through straight repayment, with the built-in buffer that if they accept low-paying work for a while, their payments will go down. For a high-income borrower, however, a decision to pay off debts rapidly involves balancing the psychological stress of being in debt against the value of having more money to invest.

Thus the financial advisors who responded to my survey may be correct in thinking that a small but significant fraction of law graduates might benefit from income-contingent repayment. However, the assessment of whether income-contingent repayment is useful for a particular borrower requires both careful analysis of the borrower's plans and circumstances and thoughtful comparisons of the results of complex mathematical calculations. Income-contingent repayment is not the best solution for every borrower, but it is of sufficient interest to warrant sophisticated understanding by more than 4 percent of the nation's law school financial aid advisors.

## THE EFFECTS OF LRAP

Up to now, we have assumed that our prototypical borrowers are at schools that have no LRAP programs. What happens if they go to a school that provides its own loan repayment assistance for their legal services work? Of course, the effects will depend on the exact rules of the particular LRAP program. Let us consider what would happen if Larry Lifer were an alumnus of Georgetown University Law Center.[23]

Georgetown expects LRAP beneficiaries to schedule repayment using a "fifteen year or more" schedule.[24] Thus, a graduate who elected twenty-five-year income-contingent repayment would qualify, but the graduate can also qualify by electing straight fifteen-year repayment. If a recent graduate's gross earnings are below a specified, inflation-adjusted "standard maintenance allowance" ($32,200 for the year 2000, and higher if the graduate lives in certain high-cost cities), Georgetown will not expect the graduate to contribute toward loan repayment, but the school's subsidy is phased out as income rises. The graduate is expected to contribute to loan repayment 50 percent of the difference of salary and standard maintenance allowance, and the student becomes ineligible for LRAP benefits when the difference of salary and standard maintenance allowance is equal to or more than twice the annual loan repayment. Loan payments due on undergraduate debt are deducted from salary for purposes of determining benefits, but undergraduate loans are not eligible for LRAP payment or forgiveness, and commercial loans are covered only to the extent that "funding allows."[25] Georgetown will "lend" the graduate the money necessary to make the monthly loan payments, and it will forgive these loans according to a specified schedule, with the total amount forgiven after five years in qualifying public interest employment. After five years, all further funds are loaned to the graduate for six months at a time and then forgiven if the borrower remained in qualifying employment for that period.

It should be noted, for purposes of analyzing the interaction between LRAP programs and income-contingent repayment, that LRAP forgiveness is not considered "income" for purposes of the income tax law.[26] It therefore does not enter the adjusted gross income calculation of the income-contingent repayment formula.

Thus, if Larry Lifer attends Georgetown, he has three plausible choices. When he graduates, he could choose LRAP and fifteen-year repayment, sticking with fifteen-year repayment even after the benefits of LRAP phase out as his income rises. His second option would be to choose LRAP and twenty-five-year income-contingent repayment at the time of graduation. His third option would be to start with LRAP and fifteen-year repayment, but switch to income-contingent repayment after about five years, as the benefits of LRAP phase out. Under all of these plans, he will pay only a small amount out of his own pocket for his first five years of legal services work. If he chooses income-contingent repayment from the beginning, his payments during the first five years will be smallest, and Georgetown will therefore lend him less money and forgive a smaller amount. Table 5.12 summarizes the consequences of these choices. I have added a fourth column to this table, showing the effects of income-contingent repayment alone without LRAP. This column simulates Mr. Lifer's situation if he were to graduate from a school with no LRAP program or if his employment (e.g., hanging out a shingle to serve working-class families) produced the same income but did not qualify for LRAP benefits.

This table shows that by electing income-contingent repayment from the beginning, Mr. Lifer will pay less out of pocket in the early years. However, if Mr. Lifer elects fifteen-year level repayment and makes somewhat larger out-of-pocket payments, the law school will pay a

**Table 5.12**

**Consequences of Electing Income-Contingent Repayment Option When Georgetown LRAP Subsidies Are Also Available (Eligible LRAP Debt Is $60,500, While Total Debt Eligible for Federal Consolidation Is $75,500; Starting Salary Is $32,000 with 4% Annual Raises)**

| Selected Repayment Characteristics | Straight LRAP (15-Year Level Debt Repayment) | LRAP with Income-contingent Repayment (25-Year Income-contingent Repayment) | LRAP with 15-Year Level Repayment for 5 Years, Then Converted to 25-Year Income-contingent Repayment for 16 Years[a] | Income-contingent Repayment Alone (No LRAP) |
|---|---|---|---|---|
| Monthly Amount Due, Year 1 | $732 (Constant for 15 Years) | $394 (Rising to $467 by Year 5) | $732 (Constant for 15 Years) | $394 (Rising to $467 by Year 5) |
| LRAP Payment, Monthly, During First Year (Loaned and Later Forgiven by Law School) | $587 (Law School Debt Repayment Only) | $317 (Rises with Income over the 5 Years)[b] | $587 (Law School Debt Repayment Only) | 0 |
| Monthly Payments Which Borrower Has to Pay out of Pocket, Year 1 (Amount Due less LRAP Payment) (% of After-tax Income[c]) | $145 (6%) | $79 (3%) | $145 (6%) | $394 (16%) (Rising to $467 by Year 5) |
| Total Subsidy Paid by LRAP, Years 1–5 | $35,220 | $20,638[d] | $35,220 | 0 |
| Debt Remaining after 5 Years | $70,432 | $82,007 | $70,432 | $82,007 |
| Monthly Out-of-pocket Payments, Year 6 (% of After-tax Income[e]) | $260 (10%)[f] | $375 (14%)[g] | $390 (14%)[h] | $488 (19%) |

[a]This option would nominally require up to 30 years of total repayment, since switching into income-contingent repayment requires starting a new repayment period unless the borrower had been paying under a plan anticipating more than 12 years of repayment. 34 C.F.R. § 685.209(c)(4) (ii)2000). However, under the facts assumed here, Mr. Lifer's income would rise rapidly enough for him to repay the debt in full, through income-contingent repayment, in a total of 21 years (5 of straight repayment and 16 of income-contingent repayment). He would receive no forgiveness at the end of that period.

[b]Because Georgetown does not cover undergraduate debt, it will prorate the portion of income-contingent repayment attributable to that debt, even though the full payment would be lower than payment of law school debt alone under fifteen-year repayment.

[c]Assumes federal income tax of $3,746 and state and local income taxes of $1,124.

[d]This is an estimate, based on 80 percent (the fraction of debt attributable to law school loans) of the $25,798 in income-contingent repayment to this point.

[e]Assumes gross income of $40,500, federal income tax of $6,062, and state and local tax of $1,808. Also assumes that Georgetown's standard maintenance allowance has risen by 2% per year and is $36,000 in the sixth year.

[f]$40,500 income less undergraduate debt repayment of $1,740 is $38,760, from which the standard maintenance allowance, which by now has become $36,000, is deducted. This yields $2,760, or $230 per month. The graduate is expected to contribute half of this, or $115 per month, toward law school loan repayment. To this must be added the $145 of undergraduate loan repayment.

greater subsidy over time, and Mr. Lifer's payments will be lower in later years. Furthermore, he will have less remaining debt at the end of five years. Thus, Mr. Lifer might reasonably elect either type of repayment, depending on his particular circumstances. Starting with fifteen-year repayment and converting to income-contingent repayment is a kind of middle option. It would keep repayment minimal when the LRAP subsidy is beginning to phase out. Under this plan, however, Mr. Lifer's debt repayments will gradually rise to $777 per month just before the debt is repaid, although at that time repayments will still be a relatively affordable 18 percent of his rising after-tax income, which will then be $53,160).[27] Under this hybrid plan, the debt will take a total of twenty-one years to repay, rather than fifteen years as in the case of level fifteen-year repayment or twenty-five years under straight income-contingent repayment.

Borrowers in other circumstances, or who graduate from law schools with different LRAP programs, might find that the balance tips more heavily for or against a particular repayment strategy. For example, after graduating from Georgetown, Cindy Civic (who plans to jump to the world of corporate law after four years in legal services) could well elect LRAP with a straight fifteen-year repayment plan, rather than income-contingent repayment, because after the first four years she would easily be able to afford the monthly payments of $732 (less than 10 percent of her after-tax income), and she would face a smaller long-term debt.

Similarly, let us change the assumption that Mr. Lifer attended Georgetown. Suppose that he attended Northwestern University Law School. Northwestern has an LRAP program, but because the program has an income ceiling of $29,000,[28] lower than Mr. Lifer's income of $32,000, Mr. Lifer could not use the LRAP program, and income-contingent repayment would look more attractive than if he had graduated from Georgetown. Or suppose that he attended American University Law School, which has a Public Interest LRAP (PILRAP) program. PILRAP is in some ways more generous than the LRAP program at Georgetown: it covers undergraduate debt and it pays subsidies as if the graduate were paying the debt over ten years, even if the graduate elects slower repayment. In other ways it is less generous; in particular, graduates receive no subsidy after their income reaches $35,000, whereas Georgetown's subsidy is phased out pursuant to a complex formula that could result in some benefits for high-debt graduates earning up to

---

[g]Because the graduate's earnings now exceed the standard maintenance allowance, the law school will pay a maximum of $115/month toward the graduate's loan repayment, which by now has grown to $490/month in income-contingent repayment. See previous note.

[h]Income-contingent payment of $535 per month in the first year of such payment, minus a law school subsidy of $145.

$60,000. Table 5.13 shows Mr. Lifer's choices as an American University graduate.

This table shows that with standard repayment, PILRAP alone will not meet Mr. Lifer's needs. He will soon become ineligible for PILRAP subsidies, so in his sixth year of work Mr. Lifer would have to pay more than a third of his after-tax income to repay his loans. Mr. Lifer has other choices, however. He could use a combination of income-contingent repayment and PILRAP subsidies to make no loan payments whatever during the first year of repayment. Indeed, he would pay virtually nothing for the first three years, during which he will remain eligible for PILRAP subsidies, and he would pay only $488 per month for his loans even in the sixth year, after PILRAP subsidies end. However, because he will owe more at the end of five years than he did when he graduated, his monthly payments will gradually rise to $925 in the final year of income-contingent repayment (19 percent of his net income, which will have risen to $58,598 annually). Or he could pay off the debt more quickly by using standard repayment for a few years[29] and then converting to income-contingent repayment. If he converted after five years, he would pay off the debt in seventeen years, and after converting to income-contingent repayment, his highest monthly payment would be $498 (in the final year of repayment).

In any event, for a student planning to use an LRAP program, creating a table modeled on Table 5.12 or Table 5.13 seems like a desirable step in financial planning. Creating tables like these could also help prospective students who plan low-income careers to choose among law schools. For example, a comparison between the two tables shows that during the first five years, Georgetown's subsidy for Mr. Lifer (based on ten-year standard repayment) would be more than three times greater than American's, and Georgetown's subsidies will continue long after the first five years, whereas American's subsidies will end.[30]

One feature of these tables should be of particular interest to law school deans at schools that lack LRAP programs. Such deans might see the federal government's income-contingent repayment plan as obviating the need for them to create such programs. However, the last column of Table 5.12 shows that in the critical early years, even using income-contingent repayment, a graduate from a school without such an LRAP program would have to pay, out of pocket, about three times as much in loan payments as a graduate from a school that has a strong LRAP program.

## THE EFFECTS OF MARRIAGE

Return to the original Larry Lifer, graduating from a school with no LRAP program and going to work for $32,000 with 3 percent annual increases. He recently graduated from law school and began thinking

**Table 5.13**

**Consequences of Electing Income-Contingent Repayment Option When American University PILRAP (LRAP) Subsidies Are Also Available (PILRAP Debt Is $75,500; Starting Salary Is $32,000 with 4% Annual Raises)**

| Selected Repayment Characteristics | Straight PILRAP (10-Year Level Debt Repayment) | PILRAP with Income-contingent Repayment (25-Year Income-contingent Repayment) | PILRAP with 10-Year Level Repayment for 5 Years, Then Converted to 25-Year Income-contingent Repayment For 12 Years[a] | Income-contingent Repayment Alone (No PILRAP) |
|---|---|---|---|---|
| Monthly Amount Due, Year 1 | $926 (Constant for 10 Years) | $394 (Rising to $467 by Year 5) | $926 (Constant for 10 Years) | $394 (Rising to $467 by Year 5) |
| PILRAP Payment, Monthly, During First Year (Loaned and Later Forgiven by Law School) | $426 | 394[b] | $426 | 0 |
| Monthly Payments Which Borrower Has to Pay out of Pocket, Year 1 (Amount Due less PILRAP Payment) (% of After-tax Income[c]) | $500 (22%) | 0 (0%) | $500 (22%) | $394 (16%) (Rising to $467 by Year 5) |
| Total Subsidy Paid by PILRAP, Years 1–5 | $11,445 | $10,775 | $11,445 | 0 |
| Debt Remaining after 5 Years | $45,402 | $82,007 | $45,402 | $82,007 |
| Monthly Out-of-pocket Payments, Year 6 (% of After-tax Income[d]) | $926 (35%) | $488 (19%)[e] | $453 (18%) | $488 (19%) |

*Note*: American University's PILRAP covers repayment of federally guaranteed undergraduate as well as law school debt. Telephone interview with Ingrid Valentine, assistant director of financial aid, American University Law School, (Sept. 21, 2000).

[a]This option would nominally require up to 30 years of total repayment, since switching into income-contingent repayment requires starting a new repayment period unless the borrower had been paying under a plan anticipating more than 12 years of repayment. 34 C.F.R. § 685.209(c)(4)(ii) (2000). However, under the facts assumed here, Mr. Lifer's income would rise rapidly enough for him to repay the debt in full, through income-contingent repayment, in a total of 17 years (5 of straight repayment and 12 of income-contingent repayment). He would receive no forgiveness at the end of that period.

[b]If a graduate were to elect a payment plan providing for slower repayment than standard 10-year repayment, American University's PILRAP would nevertheless make the same loan repayment that it would make based on standard 10-year repayment. Telephone interview with Ingrid Valentine, assistant director of financial aid, American University Law School (Sept. 21, 2000).

[c]Assumes federal income tax of $3,746 and state and local income taxes of $1,124.

[d]$40,500 gross income minus federal tax of $6,062 and state tax assumed to be $1,808 yields after-tax income of $32,630.

[e]Because the graduate earns more than $35,000, he is no longer eligible for PILRAP subsidies.

**Table 5.14**

**Effect of Marriage of Similarly Situated Partners ($32,000 Incomes, 8.25% Interest, 3% Raises, $151,000 Combined Debt Subject to Income-Contingent Repayment)**

| Selected Repayment Characteristics | Larry Lifer and Penny Lane, Unmarried Borrowers, Consolidated Amounts | Larry Lifer and Penny Lane, Married Couple | Larry Lifer and Penny Lane, Married Couple, Debt Paid in 10 Years Through 10-Year Standard Repayment |
|---|---|---|---|
| Monthly Payments, Year 1 (% of After-tax Income), Joint Return in the Case of the Married Couple, Based on Gross Income of $64,000 | $788 (18%)[a] | $879 (21%)[b] | $1,852 (42%) |
| Monthly Payments, Year 6 (% of After-tax Income), Joint Return in the Case of the Married Couple, Based on Gross Income of $76,420 | $914 (18%)[c] | $1,019 (21%)[d] | $1,852 (36%) |
| Total Payments (Current Dollars) | $342,879 | $384,645 | $222,247 |
| Present Value of Total Future Payments | $168,886 | $188,929 | $169,482 |
| Amount the Government Forgives (Current Dollars) | $141,854 | $52,387 | 0 |
| Present Value of Government Forgiveness | $34,894 | $12,796 | 0 |

[a]Assumes federal income tax of $3,746 and state and local taxes of $1,124 on each taxpayer.
[b]Assumes federal income tax of $8,725 and state tax of $2,632 on the joint income.
[c]Based on federal tax of $5,382 and state and local tax of $1,615 on each taxpayer.
[d]Assumes federal income tax of $12,247 and state and local tax of $3,674 on the joint income.
  Courtesy of Samantha Goldstein.

about loan repayment options. He is single, but he and his girlfriend, Penny Lane, are thinking about getting married. What are the consequences of marriage for their loan repayments?

First, let us consider what happens if Mr. Lifer and Ms. Lane are in roughly the same circumstances. She plans to work in legal services, with the same income. She also has the same amount of debt. Federal regulations allow the happy couple to combine their debts into a single income-contingent loan, and they require them to combine their incomes for purposes of the repayment calculation, because the government as-

**Table 5.15**
**Effect of Marriage of Differently Situated Partners ($32,000 Incomes, 3% Raises, a single $75,500 Debt Subject to Income-Contingent Repayment)**

| Selected Repayment Characteristics | Larry Lifer and Penny Lane, Unmarried Borrowers, the Debtor Using Income-contingent Repayment, Consolidated Amounts | Larry Lifer and Penny Lane, Married Couple, Debt Paid Through Income-contingent Repayment (Debt Will Be Paid off in 10 Years) | Larry Lifer and Penny Lane, Married Couple, Debt Paid in 10 Years Through 10-Year Standard Repayment |
|---|---|---|---|
| Monthly Payments, Year 1 (% of After-tax Income), Joint Return in the Case of the Married Couple | $394 (9%)[a] | $879 (20%)[b] | $926 (21%) |
| Monthly Payments, Year 6 (% of After-tax Income), Joint Return in the Case of the Married Couple, Based on Joint Gross Income of $76,420 | $459 (9%)[c] | $945 (19%)[d] | $926 (18%) |
| Total Payments (Current Dollars) | $171,439 | $111,415 | $111,123 |
| Present Value of Total Future Payments | $84,443 | $84,821 | $84,738 |
| Amount the Government Forgives (Current Dollars) | $70,927 | 0 | 0 |
| Present Value of Government Forgiveness | $17,447 | 0 | 0 |

[a] Assumes federal income tax of $3,746 and state and local taxes of $1,124 on each taxpayer.
[b] Assumes $8,725 in federal income tax and $2,632 in state and local tax.
[c] Based on federal tax of $5,382 and state and local tax of $1,615 on each taxpayer.
[d] Assumes federal income tax of $12,247 and state and local tax of $3,674.

sumes that the couple's combined income most accurately reflects one member's ability to repay debt. However, doubling both the debt and the income does not result in the same repayment schedule that the couple would have had if they had remained single, because the federal poverty guidelines, which are part of the income-contingency formula, assume that two can live nearly as cheaply as one.[31] Table 5.14 shows a comparison between the couple's situation before and after marriage; a standard repayment column is included in the table for purposes of additional comparison, although it would require them to repay an exceedingly high fraction of their income in the early years.

By marrying after choosing income-contingent repayment, Mr. Lifer and Ms. Lane will pay approximately 11 percent more in each first-year loan payment than if they had remained single, and they will pay approximately $20,000 more, over the life of the loan (measured in terms of present value), than they would if unmarried. This might be a price that they would happily pay for a combination of connubial bliss and affordable repayment.

Now consider the possibility that although Ms. Lane is, like Mr. Lifer, a $32,000 legal services lawyer, she is free of debt because she paid for her legal education out of money she saved before attending law school. If they marry, the U.S. Department of Education will attribute her income to the couple, even though she has no debt to combine with his. Compare their premarriage and postmarriage prospects in Table 5.15.

In this situation, the impact of marriage is far more dramatic in the early years of repayment. Mr. Lifer and Ms. Lane will be tempted to elect income-contingent loan repayment over standard repayment, because choosing income-contingent repayment without actually marrying could lower first-year loan repayments from 21 percent of their combined income to 9 percent of their combined income. However, by exchanging vows rather than merely cohabiting (or by remaining married rather than divorcing and living together if they have married before they notice the consequences for their loan repayments), they will (in the early years) more than double what they have to pay each month toward Mr. Lifer's student loans.[32] The "marriage penalty" of the federal student loan repayment program is thus far more severe in the early years than the "marriage penalty" imposed by the income tax law.[33] The clear message from the U.S. Department of Education to the happy couple: avoid the benefit of clergy.[34] I shall return to this marriage penalty issue in the final chapter of this book.

## NOTES

1. www.finaid.org/calculators/icr.phtml.

2. If her debts were direct federal loans to begin with, rather than FFELP loans, consolidation isn't necessary.

3. The user also enters whether or not he or she lives in Alaska or Hawaii, since the federal poverty level is set higher in those states, and the size of his family. The latter entry is necessary because the poverty level varies with the number of dependents.

4. For an explanation of why the thirty-year bond rate is recommended, see Appendix B in this book.

5. No calculator, including ours, can predict precisely a borrower's actual schedule of repayments under the income-contingent repayment option, because a borrower cannot predict in advance certain relevant events that will occur in the future, such as the rate of change in the federal poverty level (an aspect of the repayment formula) or the precise year-to-year income fluctuations of the borrower. Even if the borrower had an entirely flat rate of income increases, calculators (which assume even increases) will be imperfect predictors of the payment bills that the government's computer will send out in future years, because increases in the consumer price index and the poverty level are not the same from year to year. Even the Department of Education's own website calculator, posted to the public so that would-be borrowers can determine how much they would pay under various repayment plans, bears the following legend in bold, red, capital letters: "CALCULATIONS ARE ESTIMATES. VALUES MAY NOT REFLECT THE ACTUAL AMOUNT COMPUTED BY THE DIRECT LOAN SERVICING CENTER." The tables in this book are subject to the same caveat. We were able to check our calculator against the government's website calculator only for hypothetical borrowers whose income increased by 5 percent per annum, because that assumption is rigidly built into the government's website calculator. In that range, our calculator produces payment totals (over twenty-five years) that, measured in current dollars, are generally within one-tenth of 1 percent of the amounts reported on the government's website calculator.

6. The U.S. Department of Education also publishes an income-contingent repayment calculator on its website, at http://www.ed.gov/offices/OPE/DirectLoan/RepayCalc/dlentry2.html. However, as discussed infra, the Department's calculator is much less flexible and therefore less useful than Mr. Hsia's calculator. For example, it assumes inflexibly that the user will experience 5 percent income growth every year, and it does not show present value.

7. The Department of Education's calculator is at http://www.ed.gov/offices/OSFAP/DirectLoan/RepayCalc/dlentry2.html. A steady repayment calculator also appears on the FinAid website, at http://www.finaid.org/calculators/loanpayments.phtml.

8. The tables in this book display costs of repayment based on consolidation in late summer 2000. The FinAid website is updated annually to include in its calculations the most recently released federal poverty level values and other adjustments required by federal law. Using the FinAid calculator in 2001 will produce slightly different results than those reported here, but that calculator permits historical research by allowing the user to assume that he or she was consolidating in an earlier year. Thus, these results can be replicated by selecting the "2000" table on the FinAid calculator.

9. This is approximately the amount that would accrue during three years of law school and a six-month grace period. See Memorandum from Jeff Hanson, to Interested Parties, *Average Debt at Repayment, Law School Class of 1998—Revised*, Access Group, (Jan. 26, 2000) (on file with author).

10. For 2000–01, the Stafford loan repayment rate is the ninety-one-day treasury bill rate in May 2000 (5.89 percent) plus 2.3 percent, or 8.19 percent. This is rounded up in a federal consolidation loan to the next higher one-eighth of a percentage point, or 8.25 percent. 34 C.F.R. § 202(a)(3)(I)(E) (2000).

11. See chapter 1.

12. The mean salary for 1999 graduates starting in full-time legal services jobs was $31,795. NAT'L ASS'N FOR LAW PLACEMENT, JOBS AND J.D.'S: EMPLOYMENT AND SALARIES OF NEW LAW GRADUATES, CLASS OF 1999 at 41 (2000).

13. Letter from Juan A. Gonzalez, executive director, Legal Aid Society of Albuquerque, to the author (June 14, 2000) (on file with author).

14. Anonymous letter to the author, undated.

15. Letter from Bob Sable, director, Greater Boston Legal Services, to the author (June 22, 2000) (on file with author).

16. One of these programs gave some attorneys larger increases.

17. This assumes $6,026 in federal income tax and $1,807 in state and local income tax.

18. These directors were also identified by NLADA's Don Saunders as representative and likely to reply.

19. Assumes federal income tax of $2,996 and state and local tax of $899.

20. With an annual income of $150,000, Ms. Civic might well begin investing in stock mutual funds or other investments that historically have had long-term returns well over 10 percent. If so, her best strategy might be to elect a repayment plan through which she would pay off her student loans over the longest, not the shortest, period of time, a period of at least twenty-five additional years. Thus for a long time she would have the benefit of funds for which she was paying interest of 8.25 percent but earning interest of more than 10 percent. For just this reason, many people with mortgages elect to invest discretionary funds rather than use them to pay off their debt. On the other hand, unlike mortgage interest, only a small part of student loan interest is deductible from income tax. Thus the relevant figure for purposes of comparison is the after-tax return on investments, requiring a higher pretax return to justify this strategy of profiting on the spread.

21. U.S. Office of Personnel Management, 2000 General Schedule, http://www.opm.gov/oca/2000tbls/GSannual/html/GSDCB.HTM. This ta-

ble incorporates a locality adjustment, raising the GS level to account for the higher-than-average cost of living in the D.C. area.

22. See *supra* note 20.

23. Georgetown has two LRAP programs, both described at http://www.law.georgetown.edu/finaid/lrap.html. By virtue of working in a legal services office, Larry Lifer would qualify for the more generous LRAP I program, which is considered here.

24. If a student does not want to consolidate with at least a fifteen-year repayment schedule, Georgetown awards benefits based on a calculation that nevertheless assumes a fifteen-year level repayment amount.

25. Because commercial debt coverage is not guaranteed, this analysis assumes that it is not eligible for LRAP subsidy. This assumption also facilitates comparisons between this analysis and other analyses in this book, because income-contingent repayment does not cover commercial debt, either.

26. Taxpayer Relief Act of 1997, Pub. L. No. 105–34, § 225, 111 Stat. 788 (1997).

27. This assumes gross income in the twenty-first year, based on the 4 percent annual increases, of $72,920, federal income tax of $15,200, and state income tax of $4,560.

28. NAT'L ASS'N FOR PUBLIC INTEREST LAW, FINANCING THE FUTURE: NAPIL'S 2000 REPORT ON LAW SCHOOL LOAN REPAYMENT ASSISTANCE AND PUBLIC INTEREST SCHOLARSHIP PROGRAMS 10 at 148 (2000).

29. I have assumed conversion after five years in the table to facilitate comparison with the previous table. Mr. Lifer would be more likely to convert after three years, when the school's subsidies end.

30. This conclusion is not surprising in view of the relative magnitudes of the two programs. Georgetown's LRAP program currently dispenses approximately $630,000 annually, whereas American University's PILRAP program has dispensed $356,000 since it began in 1988. NAT'L ASS'N FOR PUBLIC INTEREST LAW, *supra* note 28, at 30, 102. Based on the size of the third-year class, Georgetown (690) is about twice as large as American (350). ABA, OFFICIAL AMERICAN BAR ASSOCIATION GUIDE TO APPROVED LAW SCHOOLS 90 at 182 (2000).

31. See the federal poverty level tables at http://aspe.hhs.gov/poverty/00poverty.htm.

32. Despite the striking differences in payment schedules in the early years, the present value of their future payments is about the same for this couple under all three plans. Note that the increased repayment obligation in the early years would be even greater if Mr. Lifer marries Ms. Lane, whose income is much greater than his; for instance, if she worked in a law firm for a salary of $150,000. If Mr. Lifer had elected

income-contingent repayment a year before meeting Ms. Lane, his options, realistically, would be either to abandon income-contingent repayment and ask his wife to make large payments on his loans (which she
might or might not be willing to do), or to refrain from marrying so that
he could continue to pay a small fraction of the couple's after-tax income
toward his loan obligations.

33. In 1999, the federal income tax on two $32,000 incomes, filed by
single taxpayers (whether or not cohabiting) would have been $7,492. If
those two taxpayers had married and filed a joint return, they would
have paid a federal income tax of $8,725, paying a "marriage penalty"
of about 16 percent of the tax due from them as single taxpayers. By
contrast, the additional student loan repayment caused by the marriage
of Mr. Lifer and Ms. Lane would be $10,584 in the first year of repay-
ment, an increase of 122 percent above the $4,752 payment required if
the couple had remained unwed. It may be worth noting that if Ms. Lane
had not married Mr. Lifer, but instead had lived with Mr. Lifer's sister,
Lisa, under Vermont's civil union law, the couple would have avoided
the additional payments required of married couples. This seems to be
a rare instance in which federal law advantages homosexual and cohabiting unmarried couples over people who are married.

34. A Department spokesperson would undoubtedly disavow this
message and suggest that this couple elect standard or graduated repayment over a shorter repayment period, since together they have $64,000
in gross income and are not impoverished. Nevertheless, the Department's regulations would permit the couple to obtain significant benefits
from income-contingent repayment, provided that the borrowers remain
unmarried.

# 6

# Why Income-Contingent Repayment Is So Unpopular

When income-contingent repayment was a gleam in the eye of policy makers, they anticipated that this option would be used by 15 percent to 30 percent of borrowers.[1] Two years later, the secretary of education projected that between 1996 and 2000, 17 percent of all direct loans, including consolidations from FFELP loans, would be repaid under the income-contingent plan.[2] In fact, fewer than 1 percent of new borrowers at schools that offer direct federal loans choose income-contingent repayment.[3] Rather than being used, as President Clinton hoped, to encourage public service, income-contingent repayment is used "mostly as a 'last resort' option [for borrowers] who have defaulted or are close to defaulting."[4] Indeed, 40 percent of its users are borrowers who were placed there involuntarily by the Department of Education after they defaulted.[5] There are no separate statistics on law student use of the program, and, as reported in chapter 4, financial aid advisors do not know how many of their students elect this option. Law students planning public interest careers might be the most likely candidates for income-contingent repayment, because legal education is among the most expensive types of graduate education and many public interest salaries are so low. The results of my surveys suggest, however, that the law students who might have the greatest interest in income-contingent repayment are wary of it, and there is little reason to think that any substantial number of them use it or even know about it.[6]

Why is there such a large gap between expectations and reality? The first answer must be that the Department of Education should probably

not have thought of the program as one that would attract as many as
15 to 30 percent of borrowers; the percentage of high-debt graduates who
think that they will have many years of low-paid work is probably far
below those percentages.[7] Furthermore, Congress and the Department
designed a program that is simply too weak to attract even 5 percent of
borrowers. The existing income-contingent repayment plan certainly suc-
ceeds in keeping loan payments affordable. Nevertheless, as the data in
chapters 3 and 4 reveal, the twenty-five-year repayment schedule fright-
ens off most of the potential customers and their counselors.[8] It affects
borrowers in several ways: by making forgiveness seem on the other side
of a lifetime, by making financial planning difficult because so many
events affecting income and expenses will intervene over such a long
period, by increasing the total amount that must be paid so greatly, and
by setting up so great a divergence with the norm of "standard" repayment.

A second part of the answer is that financial aid advisors are the critical link between the Department and student borrowers, and at least
some of them have concluded that income-contingent repayment is advantageous for virtually no law students. Recall that financial aid advisors tended to think that very few students would remain in the plan
long enough to obtain partial forgiveness, and that of those who thought
that even short-term use of the plan was not useful, the most common
reason offered was that other, less-complex repayment options were
preferable. My survey of these advisors also included an open-ended
question on which they could provide comments on the income-
contingent repayment option. Some commented that they just didn't understand the program very well, but a few comments shed further light
on the view that income-contingent repayment is simply a poor way to
deal with student debt:

> We discourage the use of income-contingent [sic] because negative
> amortization is not to anyone's benefit . . . [and] if they are still pay-
> ing on their own student loan when their children go to college it
> will reduce their ability to assist the children with college expenses.

> Financial aid counselors would encourage use of any other option
> since this one might result in negative amortization.

> A 25 or 30 year consolidation lowers the monthly [sic] nearly as
> low as an income-contingent repayment, but can save the borrower
> significant interest expense as compared to a graduated or income-
> contingent plan.

Most . . . will choose the graduated repayment option . . . as the monthly payment is similar for the first few years.

Our law graduates are [not interested in] long payment periods. Two other options are the graduated payment plan [with increasing payments over ten years] or [increasing payments over] 12–15 years.

Other options are less costly and more attractive in the long haul. I have confidence in the FFELP repayment options.

It is my understanding that by using this program they give up a lot of deferment and forbearance options that would otherwise be available to them in time of need or hardship.

To rely on an income that is going nowhere is like stating you will never be successful. [M]ost law alums want to be successful, and cannot be, if they make payments contingent on their income. A few may take advantage of this, but I bet they are doing jobs under the table and not reporting them.

These survey respondents are wise to encourage consideration of other options, but their comments may also reflect misunderstandings of the income-contingent option in relation to its alternatives. Negative amortization (increasing the principal of a loan) may indeed be to the benefit of some borrowers, if it is coupled with eventual forgiveness of the principal; also, the Department's regulations limit negative amortization, so that capitalization of unpaid interest stops when the principal balance has grown by 10 percent, and compounding of interest does not resume even after the debt is worked down. For some borrowers, simple extended repayment over thirty years may well cost about the same, over time, as income-contingent repayment. For high-debt, low-income borrowers, however, it will not lower the first several years' payments as much as income-contingent repayment, and for some of those borrowers, it will cost more in the long run.[9] Payments under the graduated repayment plan are not necessarily similar, in the early years, to those under income-contingent repayment, and graduated repayment over a long term can be the most expensive method of repayment,[10] especially compared to income-contingent repayment that includes some degree of forgiveness. The repayment options offered by FFELP lenders may be less attractive for high-debt, low-income borrowers because, while the "income-sensitive" repayment option offered by FFELP lenders may lower payments for a few years, it does not lower them as much as the income-contingent repayment option does, and it does not offer any forgiveness.[11] "Deferments"[12] and "forbearances"[13] are available under all federal repayment options, including income-contingent repayment,[14] although the reduced payments under income-contingent repayment may make them less necessary. Also, not all law graduates measure their "success" by the amount of money they make in their careers.

These comments may represent isolated overstatements, since a majority of the financial aid advisors reported in my survey that income-contingent repayment would be useful for at least 5 percent of their students. Nevertheless, one reason for the program's low use rate by law graduates may be that many financial aid advisors do not know very much about the option, and even those who think that it would be useful for 5 percent of those they advise may be so leery of the program that they actually commend it to fewer than that 5 percent.

The inherent unattractiveness of the option, the financial aid advisors' poor familiarity with the program, and the advisors' wariness of it may all have resulted from the desire of Department of Education officials to give the option a low political profile throughout the Clinton administration, despite the president's personal enthusiasm for it. FFELP lenders, eager to preserve billions of dollars of virtually risk-free federally guaranteed profit, bitterly fought against the creation of the federal direct lending program.[15] After 1993, FFELP and direct lending coexisted as competitors, and by 1998, the federal government had persuaded 20 percent of the nation's colleges to grant direct federal loans.[16] The lenders and their Congressional allies, however, spent years trying to repeal federal direct lending, or at least to prevent it from being used by borrowers at more than a statutorily fixed percentage of schools.[17] Because the "foremost" advantage of the direct lending program over the FFELP program was the availability of income-contingent repayment in the direct lending program,[18] and the lending industry feared that this repayment option would "give the direct-loan program a competitive edge,"[19] the industry targeted that plan for ridicule and attack. In 1996, three industry groups issued a report attacking the plan as too costly for students.[20] It purported to show that income-contingent repayment was "an expensive option," compared to other repayment plans, and that the Department of Education's literature gulled students into choosing this option without warning them sufficiently of the costs. Somewhat misleadingly, the report prominently featured a chart showing that for a student with a $15,000 loan and a $15,000 starting salary, all other repayment methods would be less expensive.[21] The study was circulated widely among lawmakers and financial aid advisors. It failed to persuade Congress to kill direct lending, but some observers thought that it was "remarkably effective at discrediting income contingency" and that "aid administrators became much more wary of recommending that option to their students."[22] The industry's animosity toward the federal direct lending program continues to this day. In October 2000, the Bank of America, Sallie Mae, and other industry leaders sued the Department of Education to restrain it from reducing by 1 percent the loan origination fee that students are charged when they accept a direct loan. Success in the litigation would make direct loans less attractive to student borrowers.[23]

Fear of industry and Congressional counterattacks may have caused the Department of Education to shy away from trying to make the program more attractive by forgiving loans sooner, and even from more effectively informing the public about this repayment method. Most Department officials with whom I spoke agreed to talk to me only on the condition that I not attribute their remarks to them by name or position. One told me that when the Department was developing its regulations in 1994, it never considered whether it could amortize income-contingent loans over a period shorter than the statutory maximum of twenty-five years, because "the whole program was controversial at the time, so we had no inclination to do so. And it remains controversial today, as direct lending is still under attack."[24] A former official told a reporter that the Department "has just been gun-shy [about promoting the income-contingent repayment plan] because it doesn't want to rankle any feathers with the Republicans who oppose direct lending."[25]

Politics may not deserve the entire blame for poor public relations, however. At least as presently structured, the income-contingent repayment plan would benefit only a small percentage of students, and the Department might reasonably place a higher priority on educating the public about programs affecting larger numbers of students. For whatever reason, however, the effort to make students and their advisors aware of the option has certainly diminished over the years. Shortly after the pertinent regulations were issued at the end of 1994, Department officials launched a national outreach effort to explain federal loan consolidation and its suboptions. It sent teams to universities, produced a handbook, and created a videotape. The handbook is now out of print, although its essentials are on the Department's website. The video is no longer used. The systematic visits to financial aid advisors have stopped, but they may have never reached law school advisors in any event, because the Department officials visited only the main university advisors, expecting them to pass the word to individual components of their universities.[26]

Even if the information from those briefings was passed to the law school advisors in 1995, it may not have been perpetuated to the current advisors, as there is rapid turnover and lateral movement among professionals in that field.[27] In addition, even though the Web seems to be the Department's main method for propagating information about income-contingent repayment to students, using the Web to learn about the fine print of this program or even its fairly basic information can be challenging. In July 2000, starting with the Department's home page,[28] and knowing what I was looking for, I went through six levels and thirteen clicks before I found a description of income-contingent loans.[29] Searching a different way, I eventually found the Department's calculator,[30] but it was not very helpful in computing the repayment information for Larry Lifer, Cindy Civic, or the other characters in this book. The calculator does not permit the borrower to assume an income growth rate of other than 5 percent and does not permit him or her to assume a sudden increase in income (as in the case of Cindy Civic). The Department's website also is not updated promptly, causing its calculations to be inaccurate. For example, federal poverty level figures for the year 2000 were published by the federal government in February 2000, but as of late August of that year, the Department of Education's website was still basing its calculations on 1999 poverty levels.[31] Most seriously, both the Department's calculator and its web-based chart of representative income-contingent repayments[32] display the current-dollar costs of repaying a loan under four different repayment options, but none of them discounts the stream of payments to present value. The result is that the apparent difference between the costs of ten-year repayment and income-contingent repayment seems much greater than it really is, because the user is lulled into comparing apples and oranges while thinking that one is comparing apples and apples.[33]

Besides the inherent weakness of the program, the possible disinclination of Department officials to trumpet it even to those students whom it would significantly help, and the poor quality of the Department's public information, three more factors may contribute to disaffection by advisors and students.[34] First, the program includes the horrendous marriage penalty noted in chapter 4. Many students are single when they graduate but expect to marry within a few years. They do not know whether they will marry a person with debts or without debts, but if they elect income-contingent repayment and consider marrying someone without debts, they will have to consider changing payment plans in midstream or cohabiting without marrying. This factor complicates financial planning. Second, forgiveness at the end of the twenty-five-year repayment period is presently taxable, although that could change during the two decades before anyone pays this tax. The tax is small for most borrowers, its present value is much smaller, and financial aid advisors responding to my survey did not rate this factor strongly in their reasons for skepticism about income contingency. Some of them did mention it in comments on their questionnaires, however.[35] The third factor is one that the students I surveyed ranked second in their view of why they would not want to use income-contingent repayment, and which could loom even larger over the next few years. Only debts subject to federal consolidation can be scheduled for income-contingent repayment, and commercial debt cannot be so consolidated, but commercial debt is already a significant factor for law graduates. None of our examples involving Mr. Lifer and his colleagues assumed that they had commercial debt, but many law graduates have $30,000 or more of commercial debt in addition to their Stafford loan debt. This number will rise as the cost of legal education increases, and with it will rise the percentage of debt not subject to income-contingent repayment. The standard monthly payment on $30,000 of debt is $368, nearly as much as Larry Lifer has to pay each month during the first year of income-contingent repayment on his $75,500 in Stafford loans. He could work with his commercial lender to try to schedule the payments over a longer period (escalating the total to be paid, without forgiveness), but if he does not do so, the percentage of his after-tax income that he will have to pay toward his student debts will rise from 20 percent to 38 percent, probably not a manageable amount. Even if he arranges for twenty-five-year repayment of both loans, he will have to pay 32 percent of his first-year income toward his loans. This significantly reduces the utility of the income-contingent repayment option. Larry Lifer might well decide to throw in the towel, giving up his hope of serving the poor in order to pay off the debt that he incurred so he could serve the poor.

## NOTES

1. *Analysis of Income-Contingent Loan Repayment*, APPENDIX TO U.S. DEPARTMENT OF EDUCATION, OFFICE POSTSECONDARY EDUCATION, discussion paper on Issues Relating to the Repayment of Federal Direct Student Loans, prepared for the March 1, 1994, meeting of the Direct Student Loan Regulations Negotiated Rulemaking Advisory Committee, at 3 ("it seems most reasonable to assume that the probability of choosing income-contingent repayment would increase as the savings in initial payments from doing so increased but that the probability would not be zero or one for any group. [On the assumption that the probability of choosing income-contingent repayment would gradually increase to 75 percent as the difference in initial monthly payments approached $50,] between 15 and 30 percent of borrowers would choose income-contingent repayment.").

2. *Federal Student Loan Programs: Hearing before the House Subcommittee on Oversight and Investigations of the Committee on Economic and Educational Opportunities*, 104th Cong. 327 (May 23, 1995).

3. General Accounting Office, *Direct Student Loans: Analyses of Borrowers' Use of the Income-Contingent Repayment Option*, GAO/HEHS-97–155 at 30 (Table II.2) (1997). Forty-five percent of borrowers consolidating their loans also chose income-contingent repayment, but there were only

about 60,000 consolidation loans, as of the time of the study, compared with 554,000 nonconsolidated loans. Ibid (Table II.3). The percentage choosing income-contingent repayment reported by the General Accounting Office may have been understated because the program was relatively new at the time of its study. However, as of May 31, 2000, only 1.46 percent of unsubsidized, unconsolidated Stafford loan balances were being repaid through income-contingent repayment. DOE, BUDGET OF THE UNITED STATES FOR FY 2001 373 (available online at http://w3.access.gpo.gov/usbudget/fy2001/pdf/edu.pdf, last visited Sept. 7, 2001). Of all federal direct loans in repayment (including involuntary consolidations), 6 percent by volume were loans in which, as a result of the benefits of the income-contingent repayment option, the borrower was paying less than the interest due on the loan. U.S. Department of Education, Utilization of Loan Repayment Plans in the Federal Direct Student Loan Program, http://www.gao.gov/mmsl/background.htm (last visited Sept. 7, 2000).

4. *Id.* at 2.

5. Ibid.

6. Recall that only 9 percent of the students at Catholic and Georgetown who wanted to spend substantial segments of their careers in public interest law knew much about the plan's provisions, even generally. This figure may overstate knowledge, because half of those in the 9 percent had received their information through word of mouth, which may have been inaccurate.

7. A third of the Georgetown and Catholic law students said that but for debt, they would like to spend two-thirds of their careers in full-time public service work. Even before law schools became so expensive, the proportion of graduates who followed such a career path was much lower. Aside from those who seek public service careers, it is doubtful that many high-debt borrowers expect to have low-income jobs for a long period of time.

8. As one financial aid advisor put it bluntly on a questionnaire, "twenty-five years is too long into the future for students to see a benefit."

9. See Tables 5.2, 5.3, and 5.10.

10. Ibid.

11. Sallie Mae provides a web-based calculator, at http://www.salliemae.com/calculators/repayment.html, on which a borrower may obtain information about income-sensitive (and other) repayment of Sallie Mae loans. It shows two income-sensitive plans. Under the first, Larry Lifer's $75,500 debt would be repaid over eleven years. His monthly payments during the first year would be $533 (more than the $396 under income-contingent repayment), but in the second year, his payments would balloon to $924 per month and remain there for the next ten years.

Under the second plan, he would repay the debt over thirty-one years (compared with twenty-five under income-contingent repayment). In the first year the payment would be $533 monthly, increasing to $566 in the second and subsequent years. Payments in the early years under this plan would still be larger than under income-contingent repayment, and the total payment over thirty-one years would be $210,116, larger than under income-contingent repayment using any assumption about Larry Lifer's salary increases. Compare See Tables 5.2, 5.3, and 5.10.

12. A deferment is a period of up to three years during which payments need not be made, though interest usually continues to accrue and is capitalized. They are granted for various reasons specified in the regulations; for example, while the borrower is unemployed, experiencing "economic hardship, has a graduate Fellowship, or is pursuing a rehabilitation training program for individuals with disabilities." 34 C.F.R. § 685.204 (2000).

13. A forbearance is a temporary cessation or reduction of payments approved by the Secretary of Education based on poor health, public service under the National and Community Service Trust Act, and various other reasons. 34 C.F.R. § 685.206 (2000).

14. Nothing in 34 C.F.R. §§ 685.204 (2000) (deferments), 685.205 (2000) (forbearances), or 685.209 (2000) (income-contingent repayment) prohibits this combination.

15. See generally, STEVEN WALDMAN, THE BILL (1995).

16. Stephen Burd, *Few Borrowers Repay Student Loans through 'Income-Contingent' System*, CHRON. HIGHER EDUC., Sept. 25, 1998, at A40. By volume, the direct loan program's share was even higher: 31 percent of unsubsidized Stafford loan originations ($3.4 billion of $11.2 billion) were federal direct loans. DOE, BUDGET OF THE UNITED STATES GOVERNMENT FOR FY 2001 at 372, *available at* http://w3.access.gpo.gov/usbudget/fy2001/pdf/edu.pdf (last visited Sept. 7, 2001).

17. See example, The Student Loan Privatization Act, H.R. 150, 104th Congress (1995), which would have phased out the direct lending program.

18. Stephen Burd, *Despite an Apparent Cease-Fire, the Battle over Student Loans Rages On*, CHRON. HIGHER EDUC. Jan. 24, 1997, at A19.

19. Burd, *supra* note 18.

20. NATIONAL COUNCIL OF HIGHER EDUCATION LOAN PROGRAMS, EDUCATION FINANCE COUNCIL, AND COALITION FOR STUDENT LOAN REFORM, AN EXAMINATION OF THE LONG-TERM COSTS TO STUDENT BORROWERS OF INCOME CONTINGENT REPAYMENT UNDER THE FEDERAL DIRECT LOAN PROGRAM (November, 1996), available at http://www.cslr.org/income-contingent.htm.

21. The report was fair in some ways. It acknowledged that income-

contingent repayment "can be a help to some" borrowers, and it sensibly recommended that "student loan borrowers need to be counseled thoroughly." Its critique of the Department for not providing information about the amount of forgiveness and the full repayment tables as part of its calculator was well founded, but the report was misleading in three ways. It highlighted only a single example ($15,000 debt/$15,000 income), and in this example, income-contingent repayment was the most expensive option. If the authors had either doubled the assumed debt to $30,000, or doubled both income and debt, income-contingent repayment would have been less expensive, rather than more expensive, than graduated repayment. Second, the authors counted dollars expended in twenty-five years as equally valuable as dollars expended in fifteen years, rather than discounting any of their results to present value. Third, the authors (like the government) assumed an annual income growth of 5 percent, rather than displaying the fact that income-contingent repayment becomes more valuable to the borrower as income growth rates fall below 5 percent.

22. Burd, *supra* note 18. One advisor concluded that income-contingent repayment could "double or even triple the cost of a loan" and recommends it only "as a last resort to the most desperate borrowers." Ibid. If advisors erroneously believed that the option was a good one for a large fraction of students and became more realistic as a result of the report, then it served a useful function, but if they concluded that only "the most desperate" borrowers should use it, they may have misinterpreted the authors' stated conclusions.

23. Kenneth J. Cooper, *Higher Ed: The Education Department; Lawsuit May Affect Student Loan Costs*, WASH. POST, Nov. 27, 2000, at A19, with correction Nov. 28, 2000, at A2.

24. Telephone interview with Department official, July 5, 2000.

25. Alexandra Starr, "Styron's chance," WASH. MONTHLY, May 1999.

26. Interview with Department official, June 11, 1999.

27. Collection of the data from my survey of financial aid advisors took six months, in part because so many of the advisors listed in the 1998–99 Law School Admission Council Directory were no longer in those positions in May 1999, and others left their positions at the end of the spring semester 1999 and were not replaced until later in the summer.

28. http://www.ed.gov/.

29. I clicked to student financial assistance, then financial aid for students home page, then to finding out about financial aid, then to direct loans (I had to know that the income-contingent option was part of the direct loan program), then to Publications and Guides for Students, and then to "Direct Loans: A better way to borrow" (as opposed to All About Direct Loans). Seven more clicks on the "next" button at the bottom of

the page took me to a one-page description of income-contingent repayment. Even then, I did not find the Department's calculator that would compute repayment schedules; backing up and clicking other options would eventually locate it. I could have shortened the process by clicking "search" on the home page and entering the words "income-contingent"; this would have taken me to a list of documents from which I would have made the top selection, and that would have taken me to a page about income-contingent repayment from the "Exit Counseling Guide for Borrowers." One click later, I would have found a chart with some sample income-contingent repayments, but because the incomes on the chart are only $15,000, $25,000 and $45,000, I could not have figured out Larry Lifer's repayments. I still would not have come to the calculator.

30. http://www.ed.gov/offices/OPE/DirectLoan/RepayCalc/dlentry2.html.

31. Mark Kantrowitz discovered this anomaly while creating the more up-to-date FinAid income-contingent loan repayment calculator, www.finaid.org/calculators/icr.phtml.

32. http://www.ed.gov/DirectLoan/pubs/exitborr/exb8.html.

33. Example, compare the current-dollar and present value numbers in Table 5.2.

34. A third potential negative, the requirement that borrowers permit disclosure of their tax returns to verify adjusted gross income, is not apparently a serious deterrent, at least for law students. The government already has this information, and lawyers are not likely to think that information they share with the Treasury Department should be concealed from the Education Department.

35. One said, "Primarily the taxation. Students who really need this benefit . . . will have a larger amount at the end of 25 years to be forgiven. The taxation . . . can be significant enough that the student can't pay it." Another said, "I think one of the main concerns is the taxation of the amount forgiven."

# 7

# Recommendations

Congress and the president tried to develop a program that would facilitate or even encourage public service by students who felt that their debts prevented them from undertaking it, but the income-contingent repayment option that is currently administered by the U.S. Department of Education primarily serves graduates who are on the brink of default under a different repayment plan, rather than high-debt students who want to do public service work. My recommendations begin with suggestions for students and financial aid advisors who must take the plan as they find it. I also have suggestions for Congress and the Department of Education about how they could make this option more effectively achieve the desired result.

## HIGH-DEBT LAW STUDENTS CONSIDERING LOW-INCOME JOBS

If you are thinking about spending several years in a low-income job, the income-contingent repayment option may be worth considering. Before even thinking about that particular plan, it is essential to come to grips with the more basic issue of the term of years within which you will repay your loan. Your classmates who are headed for highly paid law firm jobs will pay off their loans in ten years or fewer. Ten-year repayment may not be possible on the income that you will earn. Paying off your student debt over a period of fifteen to twenty-five years may be necessary if you want to follow the career plan you have set for your-self. There is nothing magical about a ten-year repayment period; it be-came conventional before debts were typically as high as they are now, and it is not suitable for high-debt, low-income graduates.

My surveys show that law graduates who want to do public interest work have a hard time accepting long repayment periods, and that the twenty-five-year amortization schedule for income-contingent loans is the single greatest barrier to use of this option, far outdistancing the larger total cost of repayment.[1] I also personally believe that the thought of repaying student loans so long after graduation is a daunting psycho-logical barrier, even if a twenty-five-year plan is economically advanta-geous.[2] As noted below, I think that policy makers should shorten this period. However, if you must consider a long-term repayment plan, keep in mind two factors that may make it easier to accept:

- Your education is a major asset, like a house. In fact, after a house, if you buy one, your education will probably be the most expen-sive asset you ever purchase. Since the 1930s, Americans have become quite used to purchasing valuable assets with long-term mortgages, and it makes sense for you to think of your student loan debt as the mortgage with which you purchased your edu-cation, which you have already used or will begin to use before you make your first payment. Few home buyers spend thirty years griping about having had to take out thirty-year mortgages. They are too busy enjoying their homes.[3]

- As John Kramer noted long ago, when you make debt repayments twenty years from now, you will be using dollars worth far less than the ones you hold in your hand today.[4] Long-term repay-ment plans cost more, in the long term, than short-term plans. Nevertheless, the charts that show how much more they cost, including those published by the U.S. government, are in a sense illusory, because they compare long- and short-term plans in cur-rent dollars, as if a dollar paid ten years from now and a dollar paid twenty-five years from now were equally valuable. Table 1.5 in this book shows that discounting the streams of payments to their present value, to more appropriately compare them, signif-icantly reduces the difference in their actual cost. You can gen-erate a similar table of current dollar and discounted comparisons to reflect your own circumstances.

If you are willing to consider repayment over a term longer than ten years, income-contingent repayment may be worth thinking about, but you have other options as well, and different plans will be better for different individuals. For example, you might choose graduated repayment, through which (as in income-contingent repayment), the monthly payments rise over time. On debts of at least $60,000, the graduated payments may be extended over a period as long as thirty years, but you can elect a shorter period if you can afford the monthly payments. On the other hand, for some borrowers, income-contingent repayment may be superior to graduated repayment. For example, for Larry Lifer, our career legal services lawyer, even with 7 percent annual raises, income-contingent repayment both more greatly reduces the initial payments (when he can least afford them) *and* costs less over time than 30-year graduated repayment (which keeps initial payments lower than any other alternative payment plan). See Table 5.2 in this book.

No simple formula can tell you which of the many available repayment options is best for you, but you really do have alternatives to ten-year repayment. Spending a few hours with web-based calculators could save you tens of thousands of dollars and make it possible for you to have the career you want. Unofficial calculators[5] may be better than the government's calculator, because they may permit you to make more flexible assumptions about your future income, and because the government does not compute present value, which is an important aspect of comparing plans of different durations. However, don't neglect to use the government's calculator as well, because it is the most authoritative, and if the discrepancies between the unofficial calculators and the government's calculator are significant, you should do further research to try to understand the cause of the discrepancy.[6] If the calculators show that you will benefit from forgiveness at the end of twenty-five years, don't forget to take into account the effect of possible income taxation on the amount forgiven, although Congress could eliminate the tax before then. Assume a reasonable tax rate, compute the one-time tax, and then discount the amount to its present value to see how much it would cost you in today's currency. Finally, keep in mind that only government-guaranteed debts (and direct federal loans) are subject to consolidation. To determine your full repayment obligation, analyze the repayment plans available for your commercial debt (which may include extended repayment options, but are unlikely to involve forgiveness), and add those monthly obligations to those resulting from the new federal obligation that you will assume.

If you are at a school with a good LRAP program for which the work you plan to do will qualify, it will almost always pay to use the LRAP program and then, taking that program's subsidy formula into account, to figure out which repayment formula would be best for you.[7] If your school has no LRAP program, or only a poor program that will not provide a significant subsidy, it is more likely that you will want to give the federal income-contingent repayment option serious consideration as a debt management device.

Keep in mind that a decision to consolidate your loan with the federal direct loan program and to choose the income-contingent repayment option is not permanent. You can switch out of income-contingent repayment, accelerate your payments within the option, or prepay your loan. Only borrowers who remain in the program for twenty-five years can obtain forgiveness, but borrowers who plan to do public interest work for a few years may benefit from the plan by using it temporarily to minimize loan repayments, and then switching to much more rapid repayment.[8] Other borrowers may have special circumstances warranting temporary use of income-contingent repayment. For example, a recent law graduate who is not necessarily going to have a very low income may need to sign a mortgage to buy a house. The mortgage company, looking at the student loan repayment obligations under ten-year repayment, may decide that the graduate does not qualify for its credit. The graduate might then elect income-contingent repayment to reduce the student loan repayment obligations to a minimum level, obtain a mortgage, and convert to a different repayment plan when it is convenient to do so.

Finally, unless the Department of Education accepts the recommendation of this book to change its policy of imputing all of a spouse's income to the borrower, the income-contingent repayment options will continue to contain a "marriage penalty" trap. If you elect this option and then marry, your marriage will affect your loan repayment obligations. The magnitude of the effect will be greatest if your spouse has significant income and low student debt. Your repayment obligation will be affected even if your spouse keeps his or her own money separate from yours and you have no right to spend it.

## LAW SCHOOL FINANCIAL AID ADVISORS

Financial aid advisors are incredibly important resources for law students generally, and they are indispensable in helping students who want public interest careers to figure out how to afford them. At schools with good LRAP programs, the financial aid advisors usually administer the programs, and in some cases, that may be sufficient to meet the needs of students who do not plan to go to well-paying law firms. Some jobs that would qualify in many people's minds as "public service," however, such as hanging out a shingle and serving the needs of ordinary working families, will not qualify under most LRAP programs,[9] and most schools do not have well-financed LRAP programs. Therefore, financial aid advisors need to be fully conversant with alternatives to standard repayment.

Unfortunately, most of them do not understand the details of income-contingent repayment very well (see Table 4.1), at least in significant part because the Department of Education has not helped them very much to do so (see chapter 6). My best advice is to play with the income-contingent repayment calculators and the hypothetical career plans of students for whom it might be beneficial. Financial aid advisors may be correct in thinking that most students will not remain in income-contingent repayment long enough to earn forgiveness, but advisors should note that some subsidization can occur relatively early, when unpaid interest ceases to be capitalized, and that some students would benefit by using income-contingent repayment for a few years, even if they were to obtain no subsidy at all.

Recognizing that because of its present terms, the income-contingent repayment option is helpful only for a fraction of graduates who seek low-income careers, financial aid advisors also have a significant role to play in reforming the program. Better than anyone else, they understand its value and limitations, and because of their hands-on familiarity with students' needs and this repayment option, they have credibility with Congress and with the Department of Education. Financial aid advisors (and career services advisors) should therefore be active in urging improvements in the program, both on Capitol Hill and with the secretary of education and other departmental officials.

## CONGRESS AND THE DEPARTMENT OF EDUCATION

Congress and the Department of Education must make the income-contingent loan repayment option more generous in order to achieve the goals they set in 1993 and 1994. Above all else, they must shorten the period, currently twenty-five years, during which a borrower must repay the loan before forgiveness of the remaining debt occurs.[10] This period could be abbreviated either for all users of the program or, if that is too costly, at least for borrowers who in fact have spent a long time doing public service. The period should not be so far beyond the standard ten-year repayment period that it becomes unthinkable for students who are not already at the brink of default. A fifteen to seventeen-year period seems plausible.[11]

Consider what forgiving the loan after fifteen years would do for some of the borrowers that we have considered. It would essentially double or more than double their subsidies, while freeing them from the psy-

**Table 7.1**

**Borrower Repayments and Subsidies on $75,500 Debt, Comparing Income-Contingent Repayment Plans Offering Forgiveness after 25 Years and after 15 Years (Thousands of Dollars)**

| Repayment Measurements | Larry Lifer, $32,000, 4% Raises, with Forgiveness After | | Larry Lifer, $32,000, 3% Raises, with Forgiveness After | | Lisa Lifer, $27,000, 4% Raises, with Forgiveness After | |
|---|---|---|---|---|---|---|
| | 25 Years | 15 Years | 25 Years | 15 Years | 25 Years | 15 Years |
| Payments (Current Dollars) | 194 | 97 | 171 | 88 | 162 | 77 |
| Payments (Present Value) | 94 | 63 | 84 | 57 | 77 | 50 |
| Cost or Value of Forgiveness (Current Dollars) | 30 | 79 | 71 | 88 | 83 | 100 |
| Cost or Value of Forgiveness (Present Value) | 7 | 34 | 17 | 38 | 20 | 43 |

chological burdens of twenty-five-year repayment schedules. Table 7.1 compares forgiveness after fifteen years with the current plan, for several of the hypothetical borrowers featured in this book.

Shortening the period may not require new legislation, but paying for it would require the secretary of education to reprogram other funds or to obtain an additional appropriations for the years in which the cost would be incurred. The statute provides that the period of income-contingent repayment is "not to exceed 25 years."[12] This is a statutory maximum, not necessarily also a minimum. As noted earlier, the Department did not even consider whether it had authority to provide for income-contingent loans for shorter durations. The time for such consideration is at hand. At the very least, the Department should make a careful estimate of the cost to the taxpayers of shortening the period. Because the percentage of users of this option is far smaller than the percentage estimated when the Department established a twenty-five-year repayment plan in 1994 (see chapter 6), the costs of forgiving loans must be much lower than those estimated at the time, and at least some liberality might be permitted within the original budget. In fact, there is some evidence that the program the Department created costs only 4 percent to 12 percent as much as the Department's original projection.[13] In addition, the program was created in times of budget deficit, whereas by the year 2000, legislators were having trouble deciding how to spend huge federal budget surpluses.[14] The cost to the taxpayers of reducing the period for repayment for law graduates is shown in Table 7.2, which assumes that 5 percent of all law school graduates would use an improved income-contingent repayment option. At present, virtually no law graduates use income-contingent repayment, but 2.8 percent of all law students take initial jobs as public interest lawyers.[15] In addition, some state government and private jobs offer salaries so low that income-

Table 7.2
Cost of Reducing the Period after Which Outstanding Balances Would Be
Forgiven for Law Graduate Borrowers in Income-Contingent Repayment
Option

| No. of Years after Which Debt Would Be Forgiven | Additional Annual per Cohort Cost to Taxpayers (Millions of Dollars)[a] |
|:---:|:---:|
| 19 | 3 |
| 17 | 5 |
| 15 | 8 |

[a]The Department of Education computes costs of subsidizing loan repayment in terms of annual per cohort costs. A cohort is the set of all students who borrow in a particular year.

Source: U.S. Department of Education, e-mail to the author (Aug. 31, 2000) (on file with author). The message came with the following caveat: "Estimates are provided as technical assistance only. Numbers do not reflect the policy positions or official cost estimates of the Department of Education or the Administration."

contingent repayment might be attractive. Not all of these graduates would elect any variant of income-contingent repayment, because not all students borrow, not all public service jobs are low paying, and some lawyers who start at very low salaries will quickly advance in salary (some of them joining high-paying law firms after a year or two of public service). Thus, 5 percent usage is intended to be a conservative guess.

If the income-contingent repayment plan were to be amended to make forgiveness after fifteen years available to all graduate student borrowers (as opposed to only law graduates), and 5 percent of them elected this method of loan repayment, the additional annual per cohort cost to taxpayers would be $44 million rather than $8 million.[16] To put in context this $44 million dollar annual per cohort cost of reducing the forgiveness period to fifteen years for all graduate borrowers, the annual per cohort cost of the entire Stafford loan program for graduate students is about one billion dollars,[17] lowered default rates on student loans have saved the taxpayers $18 billion since 1993,[18] and the projected budget surplus for fiscal year 2001 is $102 billion.[19]

If reducing the loan period for all users is nevertheless deemed too expensive,[20] policy makers could consider offering forgiveness at the end of a shorter period only to those who had fulfilled a public service requirement, such as having spent at least ten of the previous fifteen years in full-time public service work. To avoid controversy about what constitutes "public service" work, the term should be defined broadly; for example, full-time work for any tax-exempt organization, any agency of any level of government, any international organization (such as an agency of the United Nations or an international war crimes tribunal), or any combination of these entities.[21] If necessary to prevent abuse, an income ceiling could also be imposed; for example, forgiveness could be phased out for borrowers whose adjusted gross income, averaged over the years of the loan, exceeded specified levels.

For lawyers, the next most important reform would be to raise the annual ceiling on borrowing under the unsubsidized Stafford loan program. Students studying medicine and other health-related subjects (including public health and health administration) can already borrow $30,000 a year in unsubsidized Stafford loans (and $8,500 in subsidized Stafford loans),[22] but law students (as well as Ph.D. candidates and other graduate students) can borrow only $10,000 per year (plus $8,500 in subsidized loans).[23]

Increasing the amount of annual Stafford loan eligibility[24] would benefit all law students, because it would substitute lower-interest federally guaranteed debt, with a statutory ceiling of 8.25 percent on the interest rate, for commercial debt at interest rates that can exceed the federally guaranteed loan rate by a percentage point or more.[25] In addition, raising the annual loan eligibility limit would particularly assist high-debt, low-income borrowers who might use the income-contingent repayment option, because a larger fraction of such students' debt would be eligible for consolidation and payment through the option. Compare Larry Lifer's situation under two scenarios. Assume that he attends Catholic University Law School,[26] borrows $75,500 in Stafford loans for undergraduate and law school study, and borrows an additional $24,500 commercially over three years, at the rates prevailing in September 2000. Assume that his commercial debt is payable over twenty years, and that, as in some earlier examples, he goes to work at a starting salary of $32,000 and has annual 3 percent raises.

Table 7.3 shows that if we factor in a reasonable amount of commercial debt,[27] would-be legal services lawyer, graduating today from a private, non-LRAP law school with an average amount of indebtedness, will in the first year on the job have to pay about 26 percent of after-tax income toward the student loan, in excess of even the most forgiving estimates of what is affordable. However, simply by sweeping more of the debt into the unsubsidized Stafford loan program, the federal government could make it possible for these public servants to afford the burdens of their debt, lowering repayment, through the income-contingent option, to 16 percent of after-tax income. Furthermore, if such graduates' incomes remained low for twenty-five years, they would qualify for more than twice as much forgiveness as under the present law.

This reform also would not require new authorizing legislation but would require the secretary of education to reprogram funds or seek an increased appropriation.[28] Congress established a presumptive $10,000 annual limit on the amount of the unsubsidized Stafford loan extended

Table 7.3
Income-Contingent Repayment Option for Larry Lifer's $100,000 Aggregate
Loan, Comparing (A) the Current $18,500 Annual Limit on Stafford
Borrowing, and (B) His Situation If the Limit Were Raised So That He
Could Borrow the Entirety through FFELP or a Federal Direct Loan

| Selected Repayment Characteristics | $75,500 Debt Subject to Income-contingent Repayment, plus $24,500 Commercial Borrowing, Payable over 20 Years (Federal Repayment, Commercial Repayment [In Brackets], and Total Repayment) | $100,000 Debt Subject to Income-contingent Repayment |
|---|---|---|
| Monthly Payments, Year 1 | $394 (+$230) = $624 [26% of After-tax Income][a] | $394 [16% of After-tax Income] |
| Monthly Payments, Year 6 | $457 (+$230) = $687 [25% of After-tax Income[b]] | $457 [17% of After-tax Income] |
| Total Payments (Current Dollars) | $171,440 (+ $55,288) = $226,728[c] | $172,452 |
| Present Value of Total Future Payments | $84,443 (+ $33,077) = $117,520 | $84,705 |
| Amount the Government Forgives (Current Dollars) | $71,427 | $152,831 |
| Present Value of Government Forgiveness | $17,447 | $37,331 |

[b]Assumes federal income tax of $3,746 and state and local income taxes of $1,124.
[b]Assumes gross income of $40,500, federal tax of $6,062, and state and local tax of $1,808.
[c]To this, the commercial lender would add a guarantee fee of $1,837.50 in the 20th year.

to a graduate or professional student,[29] but it also authorized the Department of Education to raise the amount if it determines "that a higher amount is warranted in order to carry out the purposes" of the Higher Education Act "with respect to students engaged in specialized training requiring exceptionally high costs of education."[30] It can hardly be doubted that legal education involves "specialized training" or that it now involves "exceptionally high costs."[31] The secretary of education should raise the unsubsidized Stafford loan limit for law school students to the lower of $30,000 (as it is for students in the medical professions) or the actual cost of attendance at the student's school.[32] If the limit were raised for all law students, and every law student in the United States borrowed $38,500 per year in subsidized and unsubsidized Stafford loans,[33] the annual additional per cohort cost would be $69 million, compared to the $1 billion annual per cohort cost of the Stafford loan program for all graduate students. However, "if the combined volume was transferred exclusively into direct lending [i.e., if the federal government rather than banks extended all Stafford loans to law students], the savings related to the increased loan volume would more than offset the costs of raising the maximum Stafford unsubsidized amount."[34]

It might be objected that making larger loans available to law students (or to graduate students generally) would simply enable universities to raise tuition. If valid, this objection applies with equal force to all government subsidies for education, including the existing loan programs, grant programs, and education tax credits and deductions. Nobody is proposing to end those subsidies, and leading politicians often suggest expanding them.[35] In addition, the link between loan availability and tuition levels is a "hotly contested" issue, but there are apparently no studies proving that the availability of loan funds is the only factor or even a major factor in tuition increases.[36] Other factors strongly affecting tuition, particularly at law schools, include the effects of rapidly rising salaries in the private sector (which make it more difficult for law schools to retain their faculties without raising salaries), the rising costs of books and technology, the level of alumni contributions, and competition from other schools for talented students.

The Department of Education should also consider simplifying the income-contingent repayment formula. The complexity of the mathematical computations is itself a deterrent to using this program. As one Georgetown student respondent to my questionnaire put it, "Too complicated! It's easier for me to just get a firm job, pay the money, and be done with it than try to figure out how this will work over 25 years. . . . If the gov't really wished to assist me they would make it easier. After all, it's a piece of cake to take out the loan, why is the payback plan so complex?"

Three other reforms should also be undertaken. First, the Department of Education should significantly improve the quantity and quality of information about income-contingent repayment that it offers to students and to financial aid advisors. Recognizing that new financial aid advisors enter the profession regularly, and that central university officials may not communicate the full details of all federal programs to all of the advisors in particular graduate schools, the Department should develop effective materials for explaining the income-contingent option, including its advantages and disadvantages for various types of students, and make them available directly to the financial aid advisors in all of the nation's law schools and probably other types of graduates schools as well. If the repayment formula remains complex, a video, distributed either as a tape or over the Web, might be desirable. In addition, the Department should significantly upgrade its web-based calculators. It should allow students considering various repayment plans to make flexible assumptions about the rate of income growth, including the assumption that they will change careers at some point during the life of their loan. All of the Department's calculators should show present value calculations for the total cost of loan repayment, so that repayment plans of different durations can be more accurately compared.

Better information about the program should be made available not only to graduate schools but also to advisors in college financial aid and career planning offices. Some students who aspire to public service careers may be refraining from applying to graduate and professional schools, assuming that the cost of attending those institutions would frustrate their service goals. Better information about government loan repayment assistance could enable college students to make better choices about their higher education.

Second, Congress should make federal forgiveness of income-contingent loans tax-exempt. The fact that forgiveness is not tax-exempt seems to be only a minor factor, to date, in students' distrust of the program, accounting for about 1 percent of student concerns and 8 percent of financial aid advisors' concerns. However, this may reflect only the fact that any taxation is still twenty years off, or that other aspects of the program are more disagreeable to those I polled. As the program is improved, concerns about taxation could grow. It makes no sense for the federal government to give with one hand, because it has determined the beneficiaries to be needy, and take back with the other. The Department of Education and the Department of the Treasury made a joint commitment to seek Congressional repeal of the tax on forgiveness.[37] In addition, Congress has already made law school LRAP forgiveness non-taxable;[38] it should do the same for its own forgiveness program.

Finally, the Department of Education should repeal its marriage penalty on borrowers using income-contingent repayment. Ideally, it should allow married borrowers to elect to have assets and debts treated either on an individual or a joint basis.[39] Alternatively, it should regard a borrower's income as the higher of (a) the borrower's own income or (b) one-half of the combined income of the borrower and the borrower's spouse.[40] Although the Department's motive in attributing the income of both spouses to a borrower was apparently to more accurately reflect ability to pay, not all spouses share their incomes, spouses generally have expenses as well as income, and the amount of the penalty under the Department's formula can be so great that it may encourage cohabitation without wedlock, or even divorce. As Martin D. Ginsburg has shown, Sweden's tax law once did what the Department of Education has now done, simply requiring married couples to add their incomes together. The result was a rash of divorces. When the law was amended so that divorce could not free the couple from higher taxation, hundreds of thousands of Swedes began living together without the formalities of marriage, and the rate of children born out of wedlock in stable, two-parent homes soared. "It was not immorality," notes Ginsburg. "It was the idiotic tax law."[41]

The income-contingent repayment option represents a fine idea, but as a government program, it has not yet come into its own. It could be an important component of how the United States supports its young people who want to commit years, or even their whole lives, to public service. Specialized training for public service is very expensive, so a good and generous income-contingent loan repayment plan can help new law graduates to follow their hearts, but the plan we now have benefits too few, too little. American policy makers, and especially the secretary of education, should make the improvements necessary to bring into force the far-sighted program that President Clinton and Congress envisioned in 1993.

## NOTES

1. See Table 3.16. As one student put it, "A 25 year repayment is alarming when faced with the reality that this repayment will extend through the years when I may choose to have a family (possibly not working) and up to the point of retirement." Response on a Georgetown questionnaire. The twenty-five-year period may have been so "alarming" that it diverted this student from realizing that in years in which income was zero, the repayment obligation would also be zero. On the other hand, since the plan currently imputes a spouse's income to the borrower, this respondent may have understood that he or she would have to rely on such a spouse to make debt repayments during years of child rearing, and may have found that prospect too confining compared with giving up a first choice of career in favor of more rapid repayment.

2. The failure of Yale's Tuition Payment Option, an early, privately financed forerunner of income-contingent repayment, provides additional evidence that very long repayment terms for educational loans don't work well. From 1971 to 1978, Yale allowed students to borrow from the university with income-contingent repayment: for every $1,000 borrowed, they would have to pay 0.4 percent of their incomes until one of two events occurred: either the debt for their entire class was paid off, or 35 years passed. The group-based nature of the plan was designed so that wealthy graduates would subsidize those with low lifetime incomes. As a student, President Clinton himself borrowed from under this plan. Yale predicted that the debts of each class would be retired within twenty to twenty-five years, but none were. Tying debt retirement to the fortunes of the group probably killed the plan; students who planned lives of public service borrowed from under the plan, while those aiming to make a lot of money avoided it, and so there was not enough repayment to pay off the class debts. Also, as many years went by, even many graduates decided that they had paid enough, and when they defaulted,

Yale was reluctant to sue its alumni. The long-term nature of the obligation bred resentment, with one alumnus, the founder of the Idaho Yale Club, reporting that "As much as I love Yale, this is tainting my overall feelings." William M. Bulkeley, *Old Blues: Some Alumni of Yale Realize That They Owe College a Lasting Debt*, WALL ST. J., Feb. 23, 1999, at A1 (describing the program and quoting users); STEVEN WALDMAN, THE BILL 10 (1995) (Clinton's use of the program). After adverse publicity, Yale announced that it would forgive remaining debts after 2001, though it would pursue defaulters. William M. Bulkeley, *Yale to Forgive Debts, Take Loss On Old Loans*, WALL ST. J., Apr. 2, 1999, at A6.

3. Of course the asset of a legal education is less tangible than a house, and it can't be passed along to your children. However, a house can't free an innocent prisoner from death row, help to protect a crusading journalist from reprisals by a dictatorial government, restore disability benefits to an elderly person who was wrongfully denied them, or stop racial discrimination in employment. Also, your law degree could enable you to make the money needed to more rapidly repay your debt, if you ever choose to do so.

4. John R. Kramer, *Will Legal Education Remain Affordable, by Whom, and How?*, 1987 DUKE L.J. 240, 267 (1987).

5. See the FinAid calculator at www.finaid.org/calculators/icr. phtml.

6. Small discrepancies are to be expected, because people who construct different calculators may use somewhat different conventions for rounding numbers, different assumptions about what happens during the first month of repayment, or different projections about the rate of increase of the federal poverty level. Differences in outcome of more than 1 percent are worth investigating.

7. Some employers also have LRAP programs for their employees, and you could inquire about this when you interview for a job. The National Association for Public Interest Law (NAPIL) collects information on LRAP programs, and periodic consultation of its website, www.napil.org, is useful.

8. See the example of Cindy Civic, Table 5.9. As noted earlier, borrowers who believe that they can invest money to achieve an after-tax return better than their student loan rate might want to elect a much less rapid repayment plan.

9. See generally the eligibility criteria compiled in NAT'L ASS'N FOR PUBLIC INTEREST LAW, FINANCING THE FUTURE: NAPIL's 2000 REPORT ON LAW SCHOOL LOAN REPAYMENT ASSISTANCE AND PUBLIC INTEREST SCHOLARSHIP PROGRAMS (2000). A few law schools with very large LRAP programs, notably Harvard, Yale, and NYU, cover graduates earning low incomes in private practice. Ibid.

10. The statistics reported in the Georgetown and Catholic student

surveys do not do justice to the disbelief and disgust expressed in comments that respondents wrote at the end of their questionnaires; e.g., "I can't believe that anyone would sign up to the terms for the twenty-five years. Everything is weighted in the government's favor and doesn't seem a good deal for the student." "25 years is a very long time!" "2–3 years at a good firm is better than 25 years of living under debt." "The federal program seems to be a band-aid." "I don't want to be paying student loans at retirement!" "Frankly, I'm a little insulted by the tone of a 'forgiveness' program that requires 25 years. People should be rewarded for doing public interest when it is hardest—straight out of law school." "I will be 31 when I graduate, and would be VERY UNHAPPY to be paying off law school until I am 56 years old, no matter how low the payments are. My own children would be OUT of law school by that point." (emphases in original).

11. Even forgiving student loans after ten years of income-contingent repayment is not unthinkable, and it was recently suggested by experts on educational financing from the University of Missouri. "Since the income-contingent plan was conceptually developed to promote employment in low-paying public service jobs, we wonder if the current program, when the full economic impact is known, will help meet its objective. We think not. . . . We propose [that] after a maximum of ten years, the loan is closed, and no additional payments are required. . . . [A]n individual would not be saddled with a lifetime of debt and would, we think, be more likely to select public service employment. *Mortgaging Their Future, Student Debtload in the U.S: Hearing before the Senate Government Affairs Committee,* 106th Cong. (Feb. 10, 2000) (testimony of Patricia Somers and James Cofer), http://www.senate.gov/~gov_affairs/021000_somers.htm (last visited March 15, 2000). Under the Somers/Cofer proposal, some high-income borrowers might choose standard ten-year repayment because it would lead to slower repayment than income-contingent repayment, but most borrowers would probably choose income-contingent repayment because of its built-in subsidy. Thus income-contingent repayment would become the new standard norm. In their testimony, Somers and Cofer did not estimate the cost of implementing their suggestion.

12. Omnibus Budget Reconciliation Act of 1993, Pub.L. No. 103–66, § 455, 107 Stat. 312 (1993); 20 U.S.C. 1087e(d)(1)(D(2000).

13. The Department predicted that "if interest is not capitalized at all, [the program] would cost the Federal government $300 million over the cost of . . . ten year fixed loan repayment." *Analysis of Income-Contingent Loan Repayment,* U.S. DEPARTMENT OF EDUCATION, OFFICE OF POSTSECONDARY EDUCATION, *Discussion Paper on Issues Relating to the Repayment of Federal Direct Student Loans,* prepared for the March 1, 1994 meeting of the Direct Student Loan Regulations Negotiated Rulemaking Advisory Committee, at 13. Three years later, after the program was operating, the

projected cost of forgiveness was only 13.8 million dollars for the year 2021 (the first year of forgiveness), rising to 36.1 million dollars by 2030. U.S. Department of Education, Responses to Congressman Gordon's Questionnaire, in Hearing on Federal Student Loan Programs before the House Subcommittee on Oversight and Investigations of the Committee on Economic and Educational Opportunities 328 (May 23, 1995). In both cases, these projections appear to be in future dollars, so in terms of current purchasing power they are much smaller, in fact, than they might appear.

14. In 2000, the Congressional Budget Office estimated that the federal budget surplus would reach $2.17 trillion during the following decade. *CBO Projecting a Whopping $2.17 Trillion in Surpluses*, SEATTLE TIMES, July 18, 2000, at A4. The Social Security Administration was projected to have an additional $2.39 trillion surplus over the same period. Ibid.

15. NAT'L ASS'N FOR LAW PLACEMENT, JOBS AND J.D.'S: EMPLOYMENT AND SALARIES OF NEW LAW GRADUATES, CLASS OF 1999 at 13 (2000).

16. Source: U.S. Department of Education, e-mail to the author (Jan. 23, 2001) (on file with author). As in the case of the other cost numbers supplied to the author, this estimate was "provided as technical assistance only" and does "not reflect the policy positions or official cost estimates of the Department of Education or the Administration."

17. U.S. Department of Education, e-mail to the author (Aug. 31, 2000) (on file with author) subject to the caveat in note 16. The annual federal appropriation for all federal student financial assistance is currently $10.3 billion. Department of Education Appropriations Act 2000, as enacted by section 1000(a)(4) of the Consolidated Appropriations Act 2000 (Pub. L. 106–113). Thus, shortening the forgiveness period for law students to 15 years would probably increase the cost of financial aid for graduate students by less than 1 percent and would increase the cost of federal financial aid by less than one-tenth of 1 percent. The secretary of education might want to offer forgiveness after fewer years to all borrowers who had completed graduate and professional degrees and used income-contingent repayment, not just to law graduates. Of course this will be more expensive, but it may only be two or three times as costly as the numbers in this chart show, and therefore still an infinitesimal increase in the cost of the national student loan program.

18. Ellen Nakashima, *Record Low Default Rate In Student Loan Program*, WASH. POST, Oct. 2, 2000, at A2. Thus, in 1993 and 1994, when Department of Education Officials computed how much money they could afford to allocate for subsidies through the income-contingent option, they were unaware of billions of dollars that would be saved as a result of fewer defaults.

19. CBO's current budget projections, http://www.cbo.gov/showdoc. cfm?index=1944&sequence=0&from=7 (last visited Sept. 12, 2000).

20. The cost could be deemed too expensive because $8 million is

deemed an unacceptably large number. Alternatively, policy makers could determine that the author's estimate of 5 percent usage is too low, or that use of more generous income-contingent repayment by borrowers other than law graduates would excessively raise the price. It should be noted, however, that few types of graduates have debt-to-income ratios higher than those of public interest lawyers.

21. Congress has drawn a similar line in recent legislation to encourage students to perform public service. In making LRAP loan forgiveness nontaxable, Congress applied the benefit to loans forgiven "pursuant to a program of such educational organization which is designed to encourage its students to serve in occupations with unmet needs or in areas with unmet needs and under which the services provided by the students (or former students) are for or under the direction of a governmental unit or an organization described in section 501(c)(3)" of the tax law. Taxpayer Relief Act of 1997, Pub. L. No. 105–34, § 225, 111 Stat. 788 (1997).

22. In 1998, when Congress phased out the Health Education Assistance Loan Program for students in medical and related professions, unsubsidized Stafford loan eligibility was expanded from $18,500 per year to $38,500 per year for students at schools that had disbursed loans through the phased out program. See "Dear Colleague" letter from Diane E. Rogers, acting deputy assistant secretary of education for Student Financial Assistance Programs, GEN-98–18 (Aug. 1998). This authority was expanded a year later to all students in the health professions, regardless of whether their schools had participated in the program that had been phased out. "Dear Colleague" letter from Diane Rogers, chief of staff, Office of the Deputy Secretary of Education, GEN-99–21 (July 1999). Students eligible for these larger Stafford loans were those studying medicine, osteopathy, dentistry, veterinary medicine, optometry, podiatry, pharmacology, public health, chiropractic medicine, and clinical psychology, as well as those in graduate programs in health administration.

23. 34 C.F.R. § 682.204 (2000).

24. Regulations also provide for a lifetime Stafford loan borrowing limit of $138,500. 34 C.F.R.§ 682.204 (2000). This limit would not have to be changed, because three $38,500 loans would equal only $115,500, and few students borrow as much as another $23,000 as undergraduates.

25. As of July, 2000, the Access Group, a major lender to law students, charged Georgetown and George Washington students 8.594 percent on its commercial loans. The interest rate for students at the Howard Law School, or the D.C. School of Law, each a few miles away, was 9.562 percent. These rates understate the interest rate, however, because students are also charged a one-time "guarantee fee" just before repayment. In the case of a Georgetown or George Washington borrower, the fee was at least 6.9 percent (and up to 12.9 percent); in the case of Howard

or D.C. School of Law students, it was at least 7.5 percent. The interest rates vary because the Access Group starts with a rate based on the bond market and then adds a "percentage that depends on your loan program and institution." http://www.accessgroup.org (Law Access loans).

26. For such a student, the commercial loan rate is assumed to be 9.562 percent plus a one-time fee of 7.5 percent. Ibid.

27. Recall that the average total debt anticipated by Georgetown and Catholic public-interest-oriented students in 1999 was $95,000. See chapter 3, note 9.

28. Of course Congress could direct this reform itself, but Congress is not scheduled to begin to review the Higher Education Act until 2002–03.

29. 20 U.S.C. § 1078–8(d)(2)(C)(2000).

30. 20 U.S.C. § 1078–8(d)(2) (2000).

31. See Table 1–1 and accompanying text.

32. Raising it to a flat $30,000 could risk encouraging over-borrowing at some state-subsidized law schools where the annual cost of attendance is less than $38,500.

33. This is an unrealistic and very conservative assumption, because $38,500 exceeds the actual cost of attendance for in-state students at many public law schools.

34. U.S. Department of Education, e-mail to the author (Aug. 31, 2000) (on file with author), subject to the caveat in note 16. This estimate was based on the assumption that all 40,000 law students in the United States would borrow the entire $20,000 of additional Stafford funds, for an additional $800 million of loans. A $69 million dollar annual per cohort federal cost for making those loans works out to an 8.6 percent subsidy rate, and the estimated subsidy rate on all FFEL Stafford loans to graduate students, which was 5.9 percent in FY 1999, is expected to be 6.5 percent in FY 2000 and 3.8 percent in FY 2001. DOE, BUDGET OF THE UNITED STATES FOR FY 2001 at 373 (http://w3.access.gpo.gov/usbudget/fy2001/pdf/edu.pdf, last visited Sept. 7, 2001). The reason that the government could turn a loss into a profit by lending the money to law students itself, rather than paying subsidies to banks under FFELP, is that, although the default rate in unsubsidized FFEL and direct lending to graduate students is virtually the same (8.75 percent for FFEL and 8.83 percent for direct loans), the subsidy rate for FFEL unsubsidized Stafford loans to graduate students was 5.9 percent in FY 1999, whereas the profit rate on federal direct unsubsidized Stafford loans to graduate students was 13.4 percent. Ibid. Presumably, the direct loan advantage lies in not having to pay commercial lending institutions to make risk-free loans.

Another option would be for the Department of Education to raise the annual limit on Stafford loans not only for law students but for all graduate students. This would cost taxpayers still more money if the loans were extended through FFELP, or reap greater profit for taxpayers if accomplished through direct lending.

35. *The 2000 Campaign: Transcript of Debate Between Vice President Gore and Governor Bush*, N.Y. TIMES, Oct. 4, 2000, at A30 (Gore proposal for a federal tax deduction of up to $10,000 for college education).

36. *The Rising Cost of College Tuition and the Effectiveness of Government Financial Aid: Hearing before the Senate Committee on Government Affairs*, 106th Cong. (Feb. 9, 2000) (testimony of David W. Breneman, university professor and dean of the Curry School of Education, University of Virginia).

37. U.S. Department of Education, William D. Ford Federal Direct Loan Program; Final Rule, 60 Fed. Reg. 61,819, 61823 (Dec. 1, 1995).

38. Taxpayer Relief Act of 1997, Pub. L. No. 105–34, § 225, 111 Stat. 788 (1997).

39. Repeal would be consistent with the recent drive by members of Congress and the President to repeal the marriage penalty in the income tax. In the summer of 2000, Congress passed legislation to amend the internal revenue code so that married couples would no longer pay more tax than if they were single. President Clinton vetoed the bill because it would have cost nearly $300 billion over ten years, and more than half of the relief would have gone to families earning more than $100,000. George Bush, the Republican presidential candidate, supported the bill; Al Gore, the Democratic candidate, supported the veto but said that he favored "the right kind of repeal" of the marriage tax. R. G. Ratcliffe, *Spouse Tax Relief Bill Gets Vetoed*, HOUS. CHRON., Aug. 6, 2000, at 1.

40. This alternative, less favorable to borrowers, is how the major LRAP programs treat marriage for the purpose of computing the borrower's eligibility for subsidies. See NAT'L ASS'N FOR PUBLIC INTEREST LAW, supra note 11, at 107 (Harvard), 136 (NYU), 297 (Yale). Georgetown simply averages the incomes (after deducting the spouse's loan repayments from his or her gross income). *Id.* at 100.

41. Martin D. Ginsburg, *Taxing the Components of Income: A U.S. Perspective*, 86 GEO. L.J. 123, 133–35 (1997).

# Afterword

This book recommends several ways in which the income-contingent repayment option could be improved by making it slightly more generous and therefore more attractive to students who desire public service careers.[1] Unfortunately, as the book goes to press, some political winds may be blowing in the opposite direction. While neither the new administration of President George W. Bush nor Congressional leaders have made definitive statements on the subject, it is possible that the entire federal direct lending program could come under attack during 2001 or 2002. If the federal direct lending program is terminated, the income-contingent repayment option, which exists only within the direct lending program, will probably be ended rather than reformed.

Two straws in the wind suggest that the direct lending program may come under new attack. First, when the Republican leadership organized the House of Representatives in January 2001, it had to select a new chair for the Committee on Education and the Workforce. Thomas E. Petri, the Wisconsin Republican who had been an early and enthusiastic supporter of direct lending,[2] was next in line in seniority and was expected to become the committee's chair. However, the leaders passed him over in favor of John A. Boehner, reportedly because Rep. Petri had "long supported the direct-lending program that . . . many Republican lawmakers—and the bankers and student-loan-guarantee agencies that contribute to them—have sought to eliminate.[3] Lenders believe him [Boehner] to be more sympathetic to their views—a former committee staffer explained.[4]

Second, President George W. Bush appointed William D. Hansen as Deputy Secretary of Education.[5] Prior to his appointment, Hansen was the executive director of the Education Finance Council, the trade association that lobbied for non-profit lenders in the FFEL Program.[6] The Council co-authored the 1996 report criticizing the income-contingent repayment option,[7] and it had sued the Department to prevent it from lowering the fees charged to students for federal direct loans.[8]

These signs do not necessarily mean that direct lending will be attacked or that any such attack will succeed.[9] Furthermore, private lenders could try to build into FFELP an income-contingent repayment option that is more forgiving than the one that is part of the direct lending program (and, by definition, more forgiving than the income-sensitive repayment options that private lenders now offer, which provide no debt forgiveness). They could, in other words, build into private lending plans a cross-subsidy feature through which the vast majority of graduates who earn more substantial incomes, or those who enter the private sector, provide funds that could be used for partial forgiveness of loans to graduates who have low incomes, or who do public service. But private lenders generally regard their missions as providing lending services and maximizing profits, and they do not have the explicit mandate to support public service that Congress gave the Department in 1993. Therefore, if the direct lending lending program is demolished, the income-contingent repayment option may disappear into the rubble.[10]

## NOTES

1. See chapter 7.
2. See chapter 2.
3. Stephen Burd and Jeffrey Brainard, "House GOP Shuns Seniority Rules in Choosing Boehner to Head Education Panel," *Chronicle of Higher Education*, Jan. 12, 2001, p. A22.
4. Ibid.
5. Piper Fogg, "People," *National Journal*, March 17, 2001, p. 821.
6. Stephen Burd, Sara Hebel and Ron Southwick, "Cautiously Watching the President-Elect," *Chronicle of Higher Education*, Jan. 5, 2001, p. A34.
7. See *supra* note 376 and accompanying text.
8. See Burd, Hebel and Southwick, *supra* note 6 (Education Finance Council is a participant in the lawsuit); see *also* Kenneth J. Cooper, "Higher Ed: The Education Department; Lawsuit May Affect Student Loan Costs," *Washington Post*, Nov. 27, 2000, p. A 19, with correction Nov. 28, 2000, p. A2 (describing the lawsuit).
9. One Republican staff member believed that it would be "foolish" for the Bush administration to try to eliminate the direct lending pro-

gram, because that program is "withering on the vine on its own" after some prominent Universities left it. Burd, Hebel and Southwick, *supra* note 6.

10. Another possibility would be that direct lending would end, but that proponents of the income-contingent repayment option might extract, as a price of its termination, the continuation of a small federal direct lending program for the sole purpose of extending income-contingent loans, on terms such as those advocated in this book, to high-debt, low-income graduates, or to the subset of those graduates in public service. The subsidy funds would then be appropriated by Congress rather than emerging from the profits of a large federal direct lending program.

# Appendix A

# Extracts from the Law and Regulations Providing for Income-Contingent Repayment (as of January 1, 2001)

## THE STATUTE

**United States Code, Title 20, § 1087e** [the law providing for income-contingent repayment when students borrow directly from the federal government]

(d) Repayment plans.

(1) Design and selection. Consistent with criteria established by the Secretary, the Secretary shall offer a borrower of a [federal direct] loan made under this part [20 USCS §§ 1087a et seq.] a variety of plans for repayment of such loan, including principal and interest on the loan. The borrower shall be entitled to accelerate, without penalty, repayment on the borrower's loans under this part [20 USCS §§ 1087a et seq.]. The borrower may choose—

(A) a standard repayment plan, with a fixed annual repayment amount paid over a fixed period of time, consistent with subsection (a)(1) of this section;

(B) an extended repayment plan, with a fixed annual repayment amount paid over an extended period of time, except that the borrower shall annually repay a minimum amount determined by the Secretary in accordance with section 428(b)(1)(L) [20 USCS § 1078(b)(1)(L)];

(C) a graduated repayment plan, with annual repayment amounts established at 2 or more graduated levels and paid over a fixed or extended period of time, except that the borrower's scheduled payments shall not be less than 50 percent, nor more than 150 percent, of what the amortized payment on the amount owed would be if the loan were repaid under the standard repayment plan; and

(D) an income contingent repayment plan, with varying annual repayment amounts based on the income of the borrower, paid over an extended period of time prescribed by the Secretary, not to exceed 25 years, except that the plan described in this subparagraph shall not be available to the borrower of a Federal Direct PLUS loan.

(2) Selection by Secretary. If a borrower of a loan made under this part [20 USCS §§ 1087a et seq.] does not select a repayment plan described in paragraph (1), the Secretary may provide the borrower with a repayment plan described in subparagraph (A), (B), or (C) of paragraph (1).

(3) Changes in selections. The borrower of a loan made under this part [20 USCS §§ 1087a et seq.] may change the borrower's selection of a repayment plan under paragraph (1), or the Secretary's selection of a plan for the borrower under paragraph (2), as the case may be, under such terms and conditions as may be established by the Secretary.

(4) Alternative repayment plans. The Secretary may provide, on a case by case basis, an alternative repayment plan to a borrower of a loan made under this part [20 USCS §§ 1087a et seq.] who demonstrates to the satisfaction of the Secretary that the terms and conditions of the repayment plans available under paragraph (1) are not adequate to accommodate the borrower's exceptional circumstances. In designing such alternative repayment plans, the Secretary shall ensure that such plans do not exceed the cost to the Federal Government, as determined on the basis of the present value of future payments by such borrowers, of loans made using the plans available under paragraph (1).

(5) Repayment after default. The Secretary may require any borrower who has defaulted on a loan made under this part [20 USCS §§ 1087a et seq.] to—

(A) pay all reasonable collection costs associated with such loan; and

(B) repay the loan pursuant to an income contingent repayment plan.

(e) Income contingent repayment.

(1) Information and procedures. The Secretary may obtain such information as is reasonably necessary regarding the income of a borrower (and the borrower's spouse, if applicable) of a loan made under this part [20 USCS §§ 1087a et seq.] that is, or may be, repaid pursuant to income contingent repayment, for the purpose of determining the annual repayment obligation of the borrower. Returns and return information (as de-

fined in section 6103 of the Internal Revenue Code of 1986 [26 USCS § 6103]) may be obtained under the preceding sentence only to the extent authorized by section 6103(l)(13) of such Code [26 USCS § 6103(l)(13)]. The Secretary shall establish procedures for determining the borrower's repayment obligation on that loan for such year, and such other procedures as are necessary to implement effectively income contingent repayment.

(2) Repayment based on adjusted gross income. A repayment schedule for a loan made under this part [20 USCS §§ 1087a et seq.] and repaid pursuant to income contingent repayment shall be based on the adjusted gross income (as defined in section 62 of the Internal Revenue Code of 1986 [26 USCS § 62]) of the borrower or, if the borrower is married and files a Federal income tax return jointly with the borrower's spouse, on the adjusted gross income of the borrower and the borrower's spouse.

(3) Additional documents. A borrower who chooses, or is required, to repay a loan made under this part [20 USCS §§ 1087a et seq.] pursuant to income contingent repayment, and for whom adjusted gross income is unavailable or does not reasonably reflect the borrower's current income, shall provide to the Secretary other documentation of income satisfactory to the Secretary, which documentation the Secretary may use to determine an appropriate repayment schedule.

(4) Repayment schedules. Income contingent repayment schedules shall be established by regulations promulgated by the Secretary and shall require payments that vary in relation to the appropriate portion of the annual income of the borrower (and the borrower's spouse, if applicable) as determined by the Secretary.

(5) Calculation of balance due. The balance due on a loan made under this part [20 USCS §§ 1087a et seq.] that is repaid pursuant to income contingent repayment shall equal the unpaid principal amount of the loan, any accrued interest, and any fees, such as late charges, assessed on such loan. The Secretary may promulgate regulations limiting the amount of interest that may be capitalized on such loan, and the timing of any such capitalization.

(6) Notification to borrowers. The Secretary shall establish procedures under which a borrower of a loan made under this part [20 USCS §§ 1087a et seq.] who chooses or is required to repay such loan pursuant to income contingent repayment is notified of the terms and conditions of such plan, including notification of such borrower—

(A) that the Internal Revenue Service will disclose to the Secretary tax return information as authorized under section 6103(l)(13) of the Internal Revenue Code of 1986 [26 USCS § 6103(l)(13)]; and

(B) that if a borrower considers that special circumstances, such as a loss of employment by the borrower or the borrower's spouse, warrant an adjustment in the borrower's loan repayment as determined using the information described in subparagraph (A), or the alternative documentation described in paragraph (3), the borrower may contact the Secretary, who shall determine whether such adjustment is appropriate, in accordance with criteria established by the Secretary.

**United States Code. Title 20, § 1078–3** [the law permitting students who have government-guaranteed loans, but who did not borrow from the federal government, to "consolidate" (convert) those loans into federal direct consolidations loans, and repay them through the income-contingent repayment option. As indicated in chapter 2, the Department of Education allows all borrowers to make this consolidation and does not question whether private lenders' terms are "acceptable" to students who desire to consolidate.]

(5) Direct loans. In the event that a borrower is unable to obtain a consolidation loan from a [Federal Family Education Loan] lender with an agreement under subsection (a)(1), or is unable to obtain a consolidation loan with income-sensitive repayment terms acceptable to the borrower from such a lender, the Secretary shall offer any such borrower who applies for it, a direct consolidation loan. Such direct consolidation loan shall, as requested by the borrower, be repaid either pursuant to income contingent repayment under part D of this title [20 USCS §§ 1087a et seq.] or pursuant to any other repayment provision under this section. The Secretary shall not offer such loans if, in the Secretary's judgment, the Department of Education does not have the necessary origination and servicing arrangements in place for such loans.

## THE REGULATIONS

**Code of Federal Regulations, vol. 34, § 685.209** [rules for income-contingent repayment]

(a) Repayment amount calculation.

(1) The amount the borrower would repay is based upon the borrower's Direct Loan debt when the borrower's first loan enters repayment, and this basis for calculation does not change unless the borrower obtains another Direct Loan or the borrower and the borrower's spouse obtain approval to repay their loans jointly under paragraph (b)(2) of this section. If the borrower obtains another Direct Loan, the amount the

borrower would repay is based on the combined amounts of the loans when the last loan enters repayment. If the borrower and the borrower's spouse repay the loans jointly, the amount the borrowers would repay is based on both borrowers' Direct Loan debts at the time they enter joint repayment.

(2) The annual amount payable under the income contingent repayment plan by a borrower is the lesser of—

(i) The amount the borrower would repay annually over 12 years using standard amortization multiplied by an income percentage factor that corresponds to the borrower's adjusted gross income (AGI) as shown in the income percentage factor table in a notice published annually by the Secretary in the Federal Register; or

(ii) 20 percent of discretionary income.

(3) For purposes of this section, discretionary income is defined as a borrower's AGI minus the amount of the "HHS Poverty Guidelines for all States (except Alaska and Hawaii) and the District of Columbia" as published by the United States Department of Health and Human Services on an annual basis. For residents of Alaska and Hawaii, discretionary income is defined as a borrower's AGI minus the amounts in the "HHS Poverty Guidelines for Alaska" and the "HHS Poverty Guidelines for Hawaii" respectively. If a borrower provides documentation acceptable to the Secretary that the borrower has more than one person in the borrower's family, the Secretary applies the HHS Poverty Guidelines for the borrower's family size.

(4) For exact incomes not shown in the income percentage factor table in the annual notice published by the Secretary, an income percentage factor is calculated, based upon the intervals between the incomes and income percentage factors shown on the table.

(5) Each year, the Secretary recalculates the borrower's annual payment amount based on changes in the borrower's AGI, the variable interest rate, the income percentage factors in the table in the annual notice published by the Secretary, and updated HHS Poverty Guidelines (if applicable).

(6) If a borrower's monthly payment is calculated to be greater than $0 but less than or equal to $5.00, the amount payable by the borrower shall be $5.00.

(7) For purposes of the annual recalculation described in paragraph (a)(5) of this section, after periods in which a borrower makes payments that are less than interest accrued on the loan, the payment amount is recalculated based upon unpaid accrued interest and the highest outstanding principal loan amount (including amount capitalized) calcu-

lated for that borrower while paying under the income contingent repayment plan.

(8) For each calendar year after calendar year 1996, the Secretary publishes in the Federal Register a revised income percentage factor table reflecting changes based on inflation. This revised table is developed by changing each of the dollar amounts contained in the table by a percentage equal to the estimated percentage changes in the Consumer Price Index (as determined by the Secretary) between December 1995 and the December next preceding the beginning of such calendar year.

(9) Examples of the calculation of monthly repayment amounts and tables that show monthly repayment amounts for borrowers at various income and debt levels are included in the annual notice published by the Secretary.

(b) Treatment of married borrowers.

(1) A married borrower who wishes to repay under the income contingent repayment plan and who has filed an income tax return separately from his or her spouse must provide his or her spouse's written consent to the disclosure of certain tax return information under paragraph (c)(5) of this section (unless the borrower is separated from his or her spouse). The AGI for both spouses is used to calculate the monthly repayment amount.

(2) Married borrowers may repay their loans jointly. The outstanding balances on the loans of each borrower are added together to determine the borrowers' payback rate under (a)(1) of this section.

(3) The amount of the payment applied to each borrower's debt is the proportion of the payments that equals the same proportion as that borrower's debt to the total outstanding balance, except that the payment is credited toward outstanding interest on any loan before any payment is credited toward principal.

(c) Other features of the income contingent repayment plan.

(1) Alternative documentation of income. If a borrower's AGI is not available or if, in the Secretary's opinion, the borrower's reported AGI does not reasonably reflect the borrower's current income, the Secretary may use other documentation of income provided by the borrower to calculate the borrower's monthly repayment amount.

(2) First and second year borrowers. The Secretary requires alternative documentation of income from borrowers in their first and second years of repayment, when in the Secretary's opinion, the borrower's reported AGI does not reasonably reflect the borrower's current income.

(3) Adjustments to repayment obligations. The Secretary may determine that special circumstances, such as a loss of employment by the

borrower or the borrower's spouse, warrant an adjustment to the borrower's repayment obligations.

(4) Repayment period.

(i) The maximum repayment period under the income contingent repayment plan is 25 years.

(ii) The repayment period includes periods in which the borrower makes payments under the standard repayment plan and under extended repayment plans in which payments are based on a repayment period that is up to 12 years. The repayment period does not include periods in which the borrower makes payments under the graduated and alternative repayment plans or periods of authorized deferment or forbearance. The repayment period also does not include periods in which the borrower makes payments under an extended repayment plan in which payments are based on a repayment period that is longer than 12 years.

(iii) If a borrower repays more than one loan under the income contingent repayment plan, a separate repayment period for each loan begins when that loan enters repayment.

(iv) If a borrower has not repaid a loan in full at the end of the 25-year repayment period under the income contingent repayment plan, the Secretary cancels the unpaid portion of the loan.

(v) At the beginning of the repayment period under the income contingent repayment plan, a borrower shall make monthly payments of the amount of interest that accrues on the borrower's Direct Loans until the Secretary calculates the borrower's monthly repayment amount on the basis of the borrower's income.

(5) Limitation on capitalization of interest. If the amount of a borrower's monthly payment is less than the accrued interest, the unpaid interest is capitalized until the outstanding principal amount is ten percent greater than the original principal amount. After the outstanding principal amount is ten percent greater than the original amount, interest continues to accrue but is not capitalized. For purposes of this paragraph, the original amount is the amount owed by the borrower when the borrower enters repayment.

(6) Notification of terms and conditions. When a borrower elects or is required by the Secretary to repay a loan under the income contingent repayment plan, the Secretary notifies the borrower of the terms and conditions of the plan, including—

(i) That the Internal Revenue Service will disclose certain tax return information to the Secretary or the Secretary's agents; and

(ii) That if the borrower believes that special circumstances warrant an adjustment to the borrower's repayment obligations, as described in § 685.209(c)(3), the borrower may contact the Secretary and obtain the Secretary's determination as to whether an adjustment is appropriate.

(7) Consent to disclosure of tax return information.

(i) A borrower shall provide written consent to the disclosure of certain tax return information by the Internal Revenue Service (IRS) to agents of the Secretary for purposes of calculating a monthly repayment amount and servicing and collecting a loan under the income contingent repayment plan. The borrower shall provide consent by signing a consent form, developed consistent with 26 CFR 301.6103(c)-1 and provided to the borrower by the Secretary, and shall return the signed form to the Secretary.

(ii) The borrower shall consent to disclosure of the borrower's taxpayer identity information as defined in 26 U.S.C. 6103(b)(6), tax filing status, and AGI.

(iii) The borrower shall provide consent for a period of five years from the date the borrower signs the consent form. The Secretary provides the borrower a new consent form before that period expires. The IRS does not disclose tax return information after the IRS has processed a borrower's withdrawal of consent.

(iv) The Secretary designates the standard repayment plan for a borrower who selects the income contingent repayment plan but—

(A) Fails to provide the required written consent;

(B) Fails to renew written consent upon the expiration of the five-year period for consent; or

(C) Withdraws consent and does not select another repayment plan.

(v) If a borrower defaults and the Secretary designates the income contingent repayment plan for the borrower but the borrower fails to provide the required written consent, the Secretary mails a notice to the borrower establishing a repayment schedule for the borrower.

§ 685.220 Consolidation, [rules permitting borrowers who do not have federal direct loans to consolidate and obtain a federal direct consolidation loan, with income-contingent repayment terms]

(a) Direct Consolidation Loans. A borrower may consolidate one or more education loans made under certain Federal programs into one or more Direct Consolidation Loans. Loans consolidated into a Direct Consolidation Loan are discharged when the Direct Consolidation Loan is originated.

(b) Loans eligible for consolidation. The following loans may be consolidated into a Direct Consolidation Loan:

(1) Federal Stafford Loans.

(2) Guaranteed Student Loans.

(3) Federal Insured Student Loans (FISL).

(4) Direct Subsidized Loans.

(5) Direct Subsidized Consolidation Loans.

(6) Federal Perkins Loans.

(7) National Direct Student Loans (NDSL).

(8) National Defense Student Loans (NDSL).

(9) Federal PLUS Loans.

(10) Parent Loans for Undergraduate Students (PLUS).

(11) Direct PLUS Loans.

(12) Direct PLUS Consolidation Loans.

(13) Federal Unsubsidized Stafford Loans.

(14) Federal Supplemental Loans for Students (SLS).

(15) Federal Consolidation Loans.

(16) Direct Unsubsidized Loans.

(17) Direct Unsubsidized Consolidation Loans.

(18) Auxiliary Loans to Assist Students (ALAS).

(19) Health Professions Student Loans (HPSL) and Loans for Disadvantaged Students (LDS) made under subpart II of part A of title VII of the Public Health Service Act.

(20) Health Education Assistance Loans (HEAL).

(21) Nursing loans made under subpart II of part B of title VIII of the Public Health Service Act.

(c) Types of Direct Consolidation Loans.

(1) The loans identified in paragraphs (b)(1) through (8) of this section may be consolidated into a Direct Subsidized Consolidation Loan.

(2) The loans identified in paragraphs (b)(9) through (12) of this section may be consolidated into a Direct PLUS Consolidation Loan.

(3) The loans identified in paragraphs (b)(13) through (21) of this section may be consolidated into a Direct Unsubsidized Consolidation Loan. In addition, Federal Consolidation Loans under (b)(15) of this section may be consolidated into a Direct Subsidized Consolidation Loan, if they

are eligible for interest benefits during a deferment period under Section 428C(b)(4)(C) of the Act.

(d) Eligibility for a Direct Consolidation Loan.

(1) A borrower may obtain a Direct Consolidation Loan if, at the time the borrower applies for such a loan, the borrower meets the following requirements:

(i) The borrower either—

(A) Has an outstanding balance on a Direct Loan; or

(B) Has an outstanding balance on an FFEL loan and asserts either—

(1) That the borrower is unable to obtain an FFEL consolidation loan; or

(2) That the borrower is unable to obtain an FFEL consolidation loan with income-sensitive repayment terms acceptable to the borrower and is eligible for the income contingent repayment plan under the Direct Loan Program.

(ii) On the loans being consolidated, the borrower is—

(A) In an in-school period and seeks to consolidate loans made under both the FFEL Program and the Direct Loan Program;

(B) In an in-school period at a school participating in the Direct Loan Program and seeks to consolidate loans made under the FFEL Program;

(C) In a six-month grace period;

(D) In a repayment period but not in default;

(E) In default but has made satisfactory repayment arrangements, as defined in applicable program regulations, on the defaulted loan; or

(F) In default but agrees to repay the consolidation loan under the income contingent repayment plan described in § 685.208(f) and signs the consent form described in § 685.209(d)(5).

(iii) The borrower certifies that no other application to consolidate any of the borrower's loans listed in paragraph (b) of this section is pending with any other lender.

(iv) The borrower agrees to notify the Secretary of any change in address.

(v) In the case of a Direct PLUS Consolidation Loan—

(A) The borrower may not have an adverse credit history as defined in § 685.200(b)(7)(ii); or

(B) If the borrower has such an adverse credit history, the borrower shall obtain an endorser for the consolidation loan who does not have an adverse credit history or provide documentation satisfactory to the Secretary that extenuating circumstances relating to the borrower's credit history exist.

(vi) In the case of a defaulted Direct Consolidation Loan, the borrower obtains the approval of the Secretary.

(vii) In the case of a loan on which the holder has obtained a judgment, the borrower obtains the approval of the Secretary.

(2) Two married borrowers may consolidate their loans together if they meet the following requirements:

(i) At least one spouse meets the requirements of paragraphs (d)(1)(i) and (d)(1)(v) of this section.

(ii) Both spouses meet the requirements of paragraphs (d)(1) (ii) through (d)(1)(iv) of this section.

(iii) Each spouse agrees to be held jointly and severally liable for the repayment of the total amount of the consolidation loan and to repay the loan regardless of any change in marital status.

(e) Application for a Direct Consolidation Loan. To obtain a Direct Consolidation Loan, a borrower or borrowers shall submit a completed application to the Secretary. A single application may be used for one or more consolidation loans. A borrower may add eligible loans to a Direct Consolidation Loan by submitting a request to the Secretary within 180 days after the date on which the Direct Consolidation Loan is originated.

(f) [Omitted]

(g) Interest rate. The interest rate on a Direct Subsidized Consolidation Loan or a Direct Unsubsidized Consolidation Loan is the rate established in § 685.202(a)(3)(i). . . .

### § 685.202 (a) (3) (i) (E) [interest rate]

Loans for which the consolidation application is received by the Secretary on or after February 1, 1999. During all periods, the interest rate is based on the weighted average of the interest rates on the loans being consolidated, rounded to the nearest higher one-eighth of one percent, but does not exceed 8.25 percent.

# Appendix B

# Discounting to Present Value with the Long Bond Rate

A rational person would rather repay $1,000 after ten years than repay this sum tomorrow, because inflation will reduce the value of the dollar and because money that is not expended at a given moment could be earning interest or could enable the borrower to buy and enjoy the use of goods and services until it is expended. Therefore, the cost of future repayments must be discounted to the present value, particularly when a borrower is considering competing repayment plans of different durations and different payment schedules.

The present value of a stream of future repayments is quite sensitive to the discount rate selected. This is evident from Table B.1, which compares the present values of repaying $75,500 in steady monthly installments over ten and twenty-five years, using four different discount rates. The rates chosen for this table are 2.5 percent (roughly the annual rate of inflation from 1995 to 1999), 5.8 percent (the thirty-year treasury bond or "long bond" rate in late summer, 2000), 8.25 percent (the maximum interest rate on federal consolidated student loans), and 12 percent (the typical rate at which a recent graduate with heavy student debt can borrow additional money—e.g., on a credit card).

These large variations suggest the importance of selecting the most appropriate rate. A higher assumed rate will make the long-term repayment plan more attractive. For rates lower than the annual percentage rate on the loan, the higher the assumed rate, the smaller will be the reported additional cost of repaying a long-term (e.g., twenty-five-year) loan, compared to repaying the same amount of money over a short term

**Table B.1**
**Net Present Value of Repaying $75,500 at 8.25% Interest over 25 Years, with Various Discount Rates**

| Discount Rate | 10-Year Repayment ($111,123 in Current Dollars) | 25-Year Repayment ($178,584 in Current Dollars) |
|:---:|:---:|:---:|
| 2.5% | $98,363 | $133,122 |
| 5.8% | $84,738 | $95,526 |
| 8.25% | $76,476 | $77,435 |
| 12% | $66,167 | $59,044 |

(e.g., ten years). If the assumed rate is greater than the annual percentage rate on the loan, the net present value of the long-term repayment plan will actually be lower than that of the short-term repayment plan. Thus lower discount rates are "conservative" in the sense that they are less likely to make long-term loan repayment look attractive. The lowest rate in the table, the rate reflecting only recent increases in the consumer price index, is unrealistically low, however, both because the inflation rate has been unusually low in recent years and because this rate does not take into account the fact that money that is not immediately repaid can be invested (e.g., in liquid assets or in consumer goods) to produce value.

Unfortunately, there is not a single "correct" answer to the question of what discount rate a student borrower should use for the purpose of considering loan repayment. Each individual's discount rate will be different, depending on the individual's expected circumstances. In fact, each individual's discount rate will change annually, depending on changes in those circumstances.

Mark Kantrowitz, who created the FinAid website to help students analyze loan repayment, made it possible for each student using the income-contingent loan repayment calculator to insert an individual discount rate for use in present value calculations. He also offers this advice on selecting a rate:

> The discount rate should be the APR [annual percentage rate] of the highest risk-adjusted rate of return the you can obtain by investing your money, or the lowest rate at which you can borrow money, whichever is higher. The reason is [that] your decision of whether to pay off your student loan depends on whether you can earn more by investing the payoff funds in a different vehicle or spend less by refinancing the loan with a lower cost source of funds. If you have both a lower borrowing cost with a different loan and a higher investment return, the higher rate wins, because you could use the other loan to borrow money to invest, and

therefore be financially better off than you would be by paying off
the student loan. . . .

Clearly, no student would rationally accept a loan with a higher
NPV [net present value] than the amount borrowed, so perhaps the
discount rate should also be at least as much as the APR of the
student loan interest rate. On the other hand, if the student has
access to no other loans, and their highest [risk-adjusted] investment rate of return is the [risk-free] long bond (thirty-year Treasury), then the long bond is the correct discount rate to use. The
difference between the amount borrowed and the NPV could be
considered a premium the student is paying for cash flow assistance.[1]

Kantrowitz uses the current thirty-year bond rate as the default value
for net present value in the FinAid calculator.[2] In this paper, the thirty-
year bond rate has also been selected as the discount rate because it
represents a conservative point between the extremes of a low recent
inflation rate[3] and the high rate at which most high-debt, low-income
students could borrow additional funds. It could be objected that the
thirty-year bond rate is much too low a rate to use and is excessively
conservative, because no ordinary civilian (such as the graduate of a law
school) could borrow money at the thirty-year bond rate. A student using
the FinAid calculator, however, may select a higher (or lower) discount
rate.

On September 14, 2000, as this book was being completed, the thirty-
year bond rate was 5.8 percent, and that is the rate used in tables in this
book.[4] The FinAid website permits the user to find the current thirty-
year bond rate. Alternatively, see the CNN Financial Network website,
or any other convenient online financial report, for this rate.

It seems likely that the federal government will cease issuing thirty-
year bonds in the year 2001.[5] If so, the next-best measure might be the
longest-term federal bonds available in the market, or whatever other
indicator Wall Street adopts to measure the present cost of long-term
revenue streams.

## NOTES

1. Mark Kantrowitz, *Net Present Value*, http://www.finaid.org/loans/
npv.phtml (downloaded Oct. 27, 2000).

2. Another possible choice would be the historical thirty-year bond
rate, e.g., for the last ten years or the last twenty-five years. But these
measures would produce higher and therefore less conservative rates: 7
percent for the last ten years, and about 9 percent to 10 percent for the

last twenty-five years. See *The 30 Year U.S. Treasury Bill from 1977 to 1999*, STOCKMOTIONS WEEKLY MARKET NEWSLETTER, December 19, 1999, available at http://www.stockmotions.com/charts/historic30yearbond_77_to _99.htm (downloaded Aug. 24, 2000). Using a 7 percent or 9 percent rate might make long-term income-contingent and extended repayment plans seem very attractive compared to ten-year repayment.

3. Recent inflation has been unusually low, the low rate has been sustained for only a short time, and it may already be increasing. Over a long term, inflation has exceeded the current thirty-year bond rate. The average inflation rate between 1977 and 1999 was 8 percent annually. For the period from 1969 to 1999, it was about 12 percent.

4. CNN Financial Network, Latest rates http://cnnfn.cnn.com/markets /bondcenter/rates.html (downloaded Sept. 14, 2000).

5. See Jonathan Fuerbringer, *Treasury Gives 30-Year Bond a Reprieve, and Price Falls*, N.Y. TIMES, Aug. 3, 2000, at C8.

# Selected Bibliography

## BOOKS

Kolb, Charles, White House Daze: The Unmaking of Domestic Policy in the Bush Years (1998).

Phillips, Kevin, The Politics of Rich and Poor (1991).

Shapiro, Thomas N., and Edward N. Wolff. Assets and the Disadvantaged: The Benefits of Spreading Asset Ownership (2001).

Stockwell, Anne, The Guerrilla Guide to Mastering Student Loan Debt (1997).

Stover, Robert V. Making It and Breaking It: The Fate of Public Interest Commitment during Law School (1989).

Waldman, Steven. The Bill (1995).

## INSTITUTIONAL PUBLICATIONS

Access Group. Symposium on Higher Education Financing, Critical Challenges in Financing Graduate and Professional Degrees 57(1997).

Advisory Council on Family Legal Needs of Low Income Persons. Increasing Access to Justice for Maryland's Families (1992).

American Bar Association. Official American Bar Association Guide to Approved Law Schools, 2000 Edition (1999, reporting 1998–99 data).

BAUM, SANDY. GRADUATE AND PROFESSIONAL BORROWING: ARE EARNINGS HIGH ENOUGH TO SUPPORT DEBT LEVELS? (Nellie Mae Foundation) (1999).

BAUM, SANDY, AND DIANE SAUNDERS. LIFE AFTER DEBT: RESULTS OF THE NATIONAL STUDENT LOAN SURVEY (Nellie Mae Foundation) (1998).

FAMILY LAW SECTION, COMMITTEE ON THE PROBATE AND FAMILY COURT, MASSACHUSETTS BAR ASSOCIATION. CHANGING THE CULTURE OF THE PROBATE AND FAMILY COURT (1997).

GENERAL ACCOUNTING OFFICE. DIRECT STUDENT LOANS: ANALYSES OF BORROWERS' USE OF THE INCOME-CONTINGENT REPAYMENT OPTION, GAO/HEHS-97-155 (1997).

GEORGETOWN UNIVERSITY LAW CENTER. 1998 Survey of Entering Students (September 17, 1998).

KIPP, SAMUEL M., III. STUDENT BORROWING, DEBT BURDEN, AND DEFAULT: THE SPECIAL CASE OF FIRST-PROFESSIONAL STUDENTS IN THE 1990S (Access Group) (1998).

LAW SCHOOL ADMISSION COUNCIL. DIRECTORY, 1998–99 (1999).

NATIONAL ASSOCIATION FOR LAW PLACEMENT, JOBS AND J.D.'S. EMPLOYMENT AND SALARIES OF NEW LAW GRADUATES, CLASS OF 1998 at 13 (1999).

NATIONAL ASSOCIATION FOR PUBLIC INTEREST LAW. FINANCING THE FUTURE: NAPIL'S 2000 REPORT ON LAW SCHOOL LOAN REPAYMENT ASSISTANCE AND PUBLIC INTEREST SCHOLARSHIP PROGRAMS 10 (2000).

NATIONAL COUNCIL OF HIGHER EDUCATION LOAN PROGRAMS. EDUCATION FINANCE COUNCIL, AND COALITION FOR STUDENT LOAN REFORM, AN EXAMINATION OF THE LONG-TERM COSTS TO STUDENT BORROWERS OF INCOME CONTINGENT REPAYMENT UNDER THE FEDERAL DIRECT LOAN PROGRAM (November 1996).

USA GROUP FOUNDATION. STUDENT DEBT LEVELS CONTINUE TO RISE, STAFFORD INDEBTEDNESS: 1999 UPDATE 7 (2000).

## SCHOLARLY ARTICLES

Cahn, Jean Camper, and Edgar Cahn. *Power to the People or the Profession? The Public Interest in Public Interest Law*, 79 YALE L.J. 1005 (1970).

Chambers, David L. *The Burdens of Educational Loans: The Impacts of Debt on Job Choice and Standards of Living for Students at Nine American Law Schools*, 42 J. LEGAL. EDUC. 187 (1992).

———. *Educational Debts and the Worsening Position of Small-Firm, Government, and Legal-Services Lawyers*, 39 J. LEGAL EDUC. 709 (1989).

Comment. *The New Public Interest Lawyers*, 79 YALE L.J. 1069 (1970).

Friedman, Milton. *The Role of Government in Education, in* CAPITALISM AND FREEDOM (1962).

Ginsburg, Martin T. *Taxing the Components of Income: A U.S. Perspective,* 86 GEO. L.J. 123 (1997).

Hanson, Jeffrey E. *Critical Challenges in Financing Graduate and Professional Degrees, in* ACCESS GROUP, SYMPOSIUM ON HIGHER EDUCATION FINANCING, CRITICAL CHALLENGES IN FINANCING GRADUATE AND PROFESSIONAL DEGREES 10 (1997).

Kornhauser, Lewis A., and Richard L. Revesz. *Legal Education and Entry into the Legal Profession: The Role of Race, Gender and Educational Debt,* 70 N.Y.U.L.REV. 829.

Kramer, John R. *Who Will Pay the Piper or Leave the Check on the Table for the Other Guy?* 39 J. LEGAL EDUC. 655 (1989).

———. *Will Legal Education Remain Affordable, by Whom, and How?,* DUKE L.J. 240 (1987).

Michelman, Frank. *The Supreme Court and Litigation Access Fees: The Right to Protect One's Rights—Part I,* DUKE L.J. 1153 (1973).

Murphy, Jane C. *Access to Legal Remedies: The Crisis in Family Law,* 8 B.Y.U. J. PUB. L. 123 (1993).

Olivas, Michael A. *Paying for a Law Degree: Trends in Student Borrowing and the Ability to Repay Debt,* 49 J. LEGAL EDUC. 333 (1999).

Quigley, William P. *The Unmet Civil Legal Needs of the Poor in Louisiana,* 19 S.U.L. REV. 273 (1992).

Redd, Kenneth E. *Policies, Practices, and Procedures in Graduate Student Aid: A Report on the 1998 NASFAA SOGAPPP Survey,* NASFAA'S STUDENT AID TRANSCRIPT (Spring 2000).

Reno, Janet. Address Delivered at the Celebration of the Seventy-Fifth Anniversary of Women at Fordham Law School, *in* 63 FORDHAM L. REV. 5 (1994).

Wolff, Edward N. *Top Heavy: A Study of the Increasing Inequality of Wealth in America,* A TWENTIETH CENTURY FUND REPORT (1995).

Zubrow, Luize E. *Is Loan Forgiveness Divine? Another View,* 59 GEO. WASH. L. REV. 451 (1991).

## NEWSPAPER AND MAGAZINE ARTICLES

Ackley, Kate. *Til Debt Do Us Part,* LEGAL TIMES, Sept. 6, 1999, at 30, 31.

Bulkeley, William M. *Yale to Forgive Debts, Take Loss on Old Loans,* WALL ST. J., Apr. 2, 1999, at A6.

———. *Old Blues: Some Alumni of Yale Realize That They Owe College a Lasting Debt,* WALL ST. J., Feb. 23, 1999, at A1.

Burd, Stephen. *Few Borrowers Repay Student Loans through 'Income-Contingent System,'* CHRON. HIGHER EDUC., Sept. 25, 1998, at A40.

————. *Despite an Apparent Cease-Fire, the Battle over Student Loans Rages On*, CHRON. HIGHER EDUC. Jan. 24, 1997, at A19.

*CBO Projecting a Whopping $2.17 Trillion in Surpluses*, SEATTLE TIMES, July 18, 2000, at A4.

Cooper, Kenneth J. *U.S. May Repay Loans for College*, WASH. POST, Dec. 13, 2000, at A45.

————. *Higher Ed: The Education Department; Lawsuit May Affect Student Loan Costs*, WASH. POST, Nov. 27, 2000, at A19, with correction Nov. 28, 2000, at A2.

Crittenden, Jack. *Lawopoly*, Part 1 of 2, NAT'L JURIST, Feb. 1999, at 17–18.

Edwards, Ginny. *Making Public Interest Law Interesting*, PUBLIC LAWYER, Winter 1999, at 6.

Fried, Rinat. *Civil Rights Lawyer Fights Police Conduct*, RECORDER, Sept. 11, 1995, at 2.

Geraghty, Mary. *Deep in Debt, More Law-School Graduates Are Defaulting on Their Student Loans*, CHRON. HIGHER EDUC., Aug. 2, 1996, at A27.

Gray, Susan. *Lawyer's Fight against Rogue Cop Becomes Crusade for Human Rights*, CHRON. OF PHILANTHROPY, Jan. 14, 1999.

Guynn, Jessica. *For Bay Area Attorneys, Salaries in Stratosphere*, CONTRA COSTA TIMES, Feb. 19, 2000.

Hansen, Mark. *And Debt's All, Folks*, ABA JOURNAL, June 1999, at 24.

Leonhardt, David. *Law Firms' Pay Soars to Stem Dot-Com Defections*, N.Y. TIMES, Feb. 2, 2000, at 1.

McCracken, Jeffrey. *Boom Fuels Lawyer Pay Surge*, CRAIN'S DETROIT BUS., April 10, 2000, at 3.

Nakashima, Ellen. *Record Low Default Rate in Student Loan Program*, WASH. POST, Oct. 2, 2000, at A2.

Phelps, David. *Not Just Pocket Change: Local Law School Graduates Will Land Average Starting Salaries of $66,000 This Year, up 20 Percent from a Year Ago*, MINN. STAR-TRIB., April 23, 2000, at 1D.

Ratcliffe, R. G. *Spouse Tax Relief Bill Gets Vetoed*, HOUS. CHRON., Aug. 6, 2000, at 1.

Stabile, Tom. *Lawopoly: Borrowed Time* (Part 2 of 2), NAT'L JURIST, April, 1999, at 14.

Starr, Alexandra. "Styron's chance," WASH. MONTHLY, May, 1999.

*The 2000 Campaign; Transcript of Debate between Vice President Gore and Governor Bush*, N.Y. TIMES, Oct. 4, 2000, at A30.

Vobejda, Barbara. *Dukakis Student Loan Plan Gets Mixed Reviews in Theory, Practice*, WASH. POST, Sept. 9, 1988, at. A23.

Weiner, Stacy. *Speaking Up for the Mentally Disabled; Eric Rosenthal Brings Their Plight to the World*, WASH. POST, Jan. 18, 2000, at C1.

Winter, Greg. *Legal Firms Cutting Back on Free Services for Poor*, N.Y. TIMES, Aug. 17, 2000, at 1.

## STATUTES

20 U.S.C. § 1071 (2000)

20 U.S.C. § 1077 (2000)

20 U.S.C. § 1078 (2000)

20 U.S.C. § 1087 (2000)

## REGULATIONS

34 C.F.R. § 202 (2000)

34 C.F.R. § 209 (2000)

34 C.F.R. § 682.204 (2000)

34 C.F.R. § 685.202 (2000)

34 C.F.R. § 685.204 (2000)

34 C.F.R. § 685.205 (2000)

34 C.F.R. § 685.209 (2000)

34 C.F.R. § 685.210 (2000)

34 C.F.R. § 685.211 (2000)

34 C.F.R. § 685.215 (2000)

U.S. Department of Education, William D. Ford Federal Direct Loan Program; Final Rule, 59 Fed. Reg. 61,683 (Dec. 1, 1994).

## PUBLIC LAWS

Department of Education Appropriations Act 2000, as enacted by section 1000(a)(4) of the Consolidated Appropriations Act 2000 (Pub. L. 106–113).

Higher Education Amendments of 1992, Pub. L. No. 102–325, § 416, 106 Stat. 529 (1992).

Omnibus Budget Reconciliation Act of 1993, Pub. L. No. 103–66, § 455, 107 Stat. 312 (1993).

Taxpayer Relief Act of 1997, Pub. L. No. 105–34, § 225, 111 Stat. 788 (1997).

## CONGRESSIONAL MATERIALS

139 CONG. REC. S10680–81, 10729 (daily ed, Aug. 6, 1993).

Conference Report on Omnibus Budget Reconciliation, 139 CONG. REC. H6272 (daily ed, Aug. 5, 1993).

Durenberger, David. Statement on the Nomination of Richard W. Riley, 139 CONG. REC. S93 (daily ed., Jan. 21, 1993).

*Federal Student Loan Programs: Hearing before the House Subcommittee on Oversight and Investigations of the Committee on Economic and Educational Opportunities*, 104th Cong. 327 (May 23, 1995).

HOUSE COMM. ON THE BUDGET, Report 103–111, *reprinted in* 1993 U.S.C.C.A.N. 378, 480 (1993).

H.R. 2264, 103d Cong., as passed by the Senate, June 25, 1993.

H.R. 2264, 103d Cong. (May 27, 1993).

Income-contingent student loans, 138 CONG. REC. S4675–76 (daily ed., Apr. 1, 1992).

*Mortgaging Their Future, Student Debtload in the U.S: Hearing before the Senate Government Affairs Committee*, 106th Cong. (Feb. 10, 2000).

STAFF OF SENATE COMM. ON THE BUDGET, 103D CONG., RECONCILIATION SUBMISSIONS OF THE INSTRUCTED COMMITTEES PURSUANT TO THE CONCURRENT RESOLUTION ON THE BUDGET (H. Con. Res. 64) 447 (Comm. Print 1993).

Student Loan Privatization Act, H.R. 150, 104th Congress (1995).

Student Loan Reform of 1993, S. 920, 103d Cong., 39 CONG. REC. S5585, 5637–47 (daily ed., May 6, 1993).

*The Rising Cost of College Tuition and the Effectiveness of Government Financial Aid: Hearing before the Senate Committee on Government Affairs*, 106th Cong. (Feb. 9, 2000).

## WEBSITES

Access Update, "The Price of Law School: An Access Group Analysis" (Mar. 2000), http://www.accessgroup.org/update/3_2000/5.htm.

CBO's Current Budget Projections, http://www.cbo.gov/showdoc. cfm?index=1944&sequence=0&from=7.

FinAid, http://www.finaid.org/calculators/loanpayments.phtml.

———. Income-contingent Loan Repayment Calculator, www.finaid. org/calculators/icr.phtml.

Georgetown University Law Center, http://www.law.georgetown.edu/ finaid/lrap.html.

Internal Revenue Service, http://www.irs.gov.

Law Access website, www.accessgroup.org.

National Aeronautical and Space Agency's Consumer Price Index Inflation Calculator, http://www.jsc.nasa.gov/bu2/inflateCPI.html.

Sallie Mae Calculator, at http://www.salliemae.com/calculators/repayment.html.

Shapiro, Isaac and Robert Greenstein, The Widening Income Gulf (Center on Budget and Policy Priorities, 1999), http://www.cbpp.org/9–4—99tax-rep.htm.

U.S. Department of Education, Budget of the United States for FY 2001, http://w3.access.gpo.gov/usbudget/fy2001/pdf/edu.pdf.

———. "Dear Colleague" letter, GEN-99–77, June 18, 1999, at http://ifap.ed.gov/dev_csb/new/drcollg.nsf/e45795ae60c28d86852566f1005ba6ad/09cb025ddcdc3b838525679a00452b69?OpenDocument.

———. Income-contingent Loan Repayment Calculator, http://www.ed.gov/offices/OSFAP/DirectLoan/RepayCalc/dlentry2.html.

———. Student Financial Assistance Policy, Indicator 1.4, http://www.ed.gov/pubs/AnnualPlan 2001/069-red.pdf.

U.S. Department of Health and Human Services, Poverty Guidelines for 2000, http://aspe.hhs.gov/poverty/00poverty.htm.

U.S. General Accounting Office, Utilization of Loan Repayment Plans in the Federal Direct Student Loan Program, http://www.gao.gov/mmsl/background.htm.

U.S. News and World Report, Law School Comparison Tables, http://www.usnews.com/usnews/edu/beyond/grad/gradlaw.htm.

U.S. Office of Personnel Management, http://www.opm.gov/oca/2000tbls/GSannual/html/GSDCB.htm.

White House Press Release, "The Clinton-Gore Administration: Making College More Affordable and Accessible for America's Families," http://www.pub.whitehouse.gov/uri-res/I2R?urn:pdi://oma.eop.gov.us/2000/8/10/8.text.

# Index

## ABOUT THE AUTHOR

PHILIP G. SCHRAG is a Professor of Law and Director of the Center for Applied Legal Studies at Georgetown University. A graduate of Harvard College and Yale Law School, he was an Assistant Counsel of the NAACP Legal Defense and Educational Fund and was the first Consumer Advocate of the City of New York before he began a career in teaching law. During the administration of President Jimmy Carter, he served as the Deputy General Counsel of the United States Arms Control and Disarmament Agency. At Georgetown, he teaches a course in litigation and supervises students who earn course credit and learn advocacy by representing refugees from political and religious persecution who seek asylum in the United States. He also directs the Public Interest Law Scholars Program, which offers scholarship assistance and academic enrichment to a small number of competitively selected students who plan to spend their lives in public service. This is his eleventh book.